The Primal Whimper

More Readings from the *Journal of Polymorphous Perversity*®

Other books by the author

Oral Sadism and the Vegetarian Personality
The Directory of Humor Magazines and Humor Organizations in
  America and Canada

The Primal Whimper

More Readings from the *Journal of Polymorphous Perversity*®

edited by
Glenn C. Ellenbogen, Ph.D.

A STONESONG PRESS BOOK

Ballantine Books   New York

To Sigmund Freud, Woody Allen, and Marty Obler—
three wild and crazy guys.

Contents

Preface

Way back in the '70s, when I was a graduate student in psychology, I discovered that the field of psychology and the psychologists, psychiatrists, and other mental health workers who inhabited it were a bit too serious. What was missing was some healthy, lighthearted perspective—humor. At first, I dealt with this discovery, and my desire to foster some healthy, lighthearted perspective in the field, by simply writing humorous spoofs of psychology and getting them published in magazines which no doubt reached few in the field of psychology. In 1980, with the receipt of my doctorate, I founded Wry-Bred Press, a small publishing house devoted specifically to the publication and distribution of humorous and satirical works in psychology.

Between 1980 and 1983, I authored and Wry-Bred Press published several "monographs," beginning with "The Scale of Mental Abilities Requiring Thinking Somewhat (S.M.A.R.T.S.)," a parody of the Wechsler intelligence tests. The monographs, published under the fictitious banner of the "Journal of Polymorphous Perversity," slowly made their way into the field and I started to receive not only letters of encouragement but *submissions* for publication in "your journal." Of course, receipt of submissions for publication in my "journal" was in itself humorous, since there was no *real* "Journal of Polymorphous Perversity." Both logic and mental health dictated that I should start a real journal to publish these humorous submissions so, in 1984, Wry-Bred Press released the first issue of the new psychology humor magazine, not surprisingly entitled the *Journal of Polymorphous Perversity*.

As issue after issue of the *Journal of Polymorphous Perversity* spread through the field, I began to see encouraging signs that the magazine was having an impact on psychology, helping psychologists and their brethren to lighten up a bit. State and regional psychological associations began seeking permission from Wry-Bred Press to reprint articles from the *Journal of Polymorphous Perversity* in their official magazines and newsletters. Some reprints from the *Journal of Polymorphous Perversity* began creeping their way into intro psychology textbooks. I began receiving personal invitations to address the members of *serious* state and regional psychological associations on the topic of humor, which I obliged with such appropriate and tasteful talks as "Humor in the Psychiatric Emergency Room and the Rest of Life." And then, Brunner/Mazel Publishers, one of the leading *serious* publishers of scholarly psychology and psychiatry texts, invited me to put together an anthology of articles from the *Journal of Polymorphous Perversity*. This was indeed making serious inroads in injecting a dose of humorous medicine into the field of psychology!

In 1986, Brunner/Mazel released the *Journal of Polymorphous Perversity* anthology—*Oral Sadism and the Vegetarian Personality*. It still remained to be seen how Brunner/Mazel's courageous gamble in publishing the book would fare, whether humor would appeal to the *serious* psychology book-buying market. To my relief (and no doubt Brunner/Mazel's as well), the book was indeed accepted (if not embraced) by the psychological community long accustomed to consuming *serious*, dry, oftentimes stodgy psychological texts. Soon thereafter, German- and Japanese-language editions of *Oral Sadism and the Vegetarian Personality* were published. To date, there are more than 50,000 copies of the book in print and it continues to sell.

Which brings us to 1989. I think that it is fair to say that the *Journal of Polymorphous Perversity* has made significant progress in helping to provide psychology with a tinge of lighthearted, humorous perspective. However, there is certainly more work to be done. A second assault upon all that is serious in psychology is required to reinforce the healthy, therapeutic dose of humorous perspective provided by *Oral Sadism and the Vegetarian Personality*. That assault comes in the form of this second anthology of *Journal of Polymorphous Perversity* articles—*The Primal Whimper*. Hopefully, this volume, too, will continue helping psychologists and their brethren in becoming less serious and in taking humor more seriously.

Glenn C. Ellenbogen
New York, New York

Acknowledgments

I would like to gratefully acknowledge the help of the following *Journal of Polymorphous Perversity*® associate editors, each of whom was kind enough to review the many manuscripts that I forwarded to them for review when the topic touched upon their specialty area:

Milton Spett, Ph.D. (Clinical Psychology), Edward E. Coons, Ph.D. (Comparative/Physiological Psychology), Gregory N. Reising, Ph.D. (Counseling Psychology), Les Halpert, Ph.D. (Developmental Psychology), George E. Rowland, Ph.D. (Engineering Psychology), Richard J. Koppenaal, Ph.D. (Experimental Psychology), James F. Harper, Ph.D. (Forensic Psychology), Robert Perloff, Ph.D. (Industrial/Organizational Psychology), Gordon D. Wolf, Ph.D. (Medical Psychology), Charles F. Levinthal, Ph.D. (Neuropsychology), Christine Holle, M.S.N. (Psychiatric Nursing), Benjamin Strouse, M.S.W. (Psychiatric Social Work), Robert S. Hoffman, M.D. (Psychiatry and Neurology), Estelle Wade, Ph.D. (Psychoanalysis), E. M. Bard, Ph.D. (School Psychology), George Quattrone, Ph.D. (Social Psychology), David O. Herman, Ph.D. (Tests and Measurements).

The decision as to what constitutes "good" humor involves a very subjective process. Thus, the associate editors were rarely in agreement, either among themselves or with me, about which articles merited publication. The responsibility for making the final selections for inclusion in both the regular journal issues and this anthology was ultimately mine and mine alone. The presence of any given article in this anthology should not be construed as reflecting the endorsement of the associate editors.

Lastly, I would like to thank the many authors whose works appear in this anthology.

The Primal Whimper

More Readings from the *Journal of Polymorphous Perversity*®

1
Psychotherapy

Maximum Security Amusement Parks (M-SAPs): A Modest Proposal for the Treatment of Adolescence

Lawrence G. Calhoun, Ph.D., W. Scott Terry, Ph.D., and Arnie Cann, Ph.D
University of North Carolina at Charlotte

As we have argued elsewhere (Calhoun, Cann, & Terry, 1988), and as everybody already knows, adolescence *is* a disease. While it apparently is not contagious, it can engender other disorders. For example, adolescence in a child can cause mental illness in a parent. However, in spite of the universal recognition that adolescence is a sickness that has existed for many years, there is still no useful treatment for this condition. While this may be a result of the failure of any major celebrity to adopt this disease and have a telethon for it, it is nevertheless a failure that must be addressed.

While psychopathy and adolescence are not the same disorder, the successful treatment of psychopathy may suggest potential interventions for adolescence. The most effective treatment for psychopathy is aging (Davison & Neale, 1986). Unfortunately, parents age much more quickly than do adolescents and (unless one is a parent of an adolescent) aging usually takes a long time. We can't wait any more.

Our proposal is the creation of "amusement parks" modelled on "Micky World," but with certain features which those sorts of "amusement" parks do not have. In our terminology, we refer to these proposed treatment centers as Maximum Security Amusement Parks (M-SAPs). While our experience and that of the millions of other persons who are currently standing in line at "Micky World" (and other such locations) suggest that similar treatment centers already exist (see the state map of Florida for specific locations), we propose specialized treatment centers.

As we envision them, M-SAPs will be available throughout the United States, with at least one center within a 10-minute drive of the home of the parent of any adolescent. This is to make it easy to get there and for parents to be able to say *Yes* when the child asks, "Are we there yet?" A brief screening process for the diagnosis of adolescence will be used, and the following criteria will be employed:

    a. **Chronological age between 13 and 21?**
       If yes, automatically qualifies for diagnosis.
    b. **Mental age between 13 and 21?**
       If yes, automatically qualifies for diagnosis.
    c. **Uses the word "car" more than 1,000 times in a week's span?**
       If yes, automatically qualifies for a bus ticket to M-SAP.
    d. **Knows the ending to all your "back when I was a child . . ." stories and repeats them along with you?**
       If yes, automatically qualifies for an airline ticket to M-SAP.
    e. **Does the child suggest you don't really know what rock 'n' roll is?**
       If yes, automatically qualifies for admission to M-SAP plus the child receives a cassette player to take with him/her and one tape—"The Turtles' Greatest Hits!"

Only adolescents will be admitted to such centers, due to the potential danger of cross-disease contagion. The M-SAPs will include a wide variety of rides, fake animals, people dressed up to look like fake animals, lines, plastic decorations, and more lines. These qualities of "amusement" parks are known to hasten aging in normal adults, and it is hoped that M-SAPs will have the same effect on adolescents. Adolescents who eventually do become tired and bored (in adolescence boredom sets in within 10 minutes of admission) will be allowed to leave the park in 10 years, when they become mentally 21, or when they reach the exit after waiting in yet another line—whichever of these three comes first (10 years usually passes first).

The M-SAPs will of course need some special attractions not available in regular amusement parks. On each corner there will be a bathroom with large mirrors and blow dryers. All clothing will be disposable and biodegradable, since adolescents won't wear anything that's been worn once already. The bumper cars will all look like Trans Ams or IROCs. The roller coasters will have a pizza stand near the entrance and an ice-cream sundae stand at the exit (the roller coaster itself will be constructed of washable plastic).

While this may sound like another liberal proposal for prison furloughs in reverse, with a large price tag requiring an increase in taxes, these assumptions are false. The program will *not* require any public moneys. First, adolescents will of course be required to pay admission—to be calculated based on what it costs at "Micky World" for 3 days, including meals, hotel, rides, and exit permits, and assumed to be in the neighborhood of half of a 4-year undergraduate education at any Ivy League university. Second, donations will pour in from parents, neighbors, high school teachers, peace officers, and normal persons. Third, and this is most crucial, adolescents will voluntarily enter and stay in the M-SAPs because part of the syndrome is to regard places like this as good places to be.

In sum, Maximum Security Amusement Parks for the treatment of adolescence are the alternative of choice for several reasons. They encourage aging and retain victims until enough aging has occurred to induce a cure, and are fiscally conservative and likely to show a profit. Plus, they are likely to lead to a great decrease in the level of mental illness in the general adult population because adolescence, the only known source of cross-disease contagion, will be quarantined in the Maximum Security Amusement Parks.

References

Calhoun, L. G., Cann, A., & Terry, W. S. (1988). *Adolescence is too a disease!* Unpublishable manuscript.

Davison, G. C., & Neale, J. M. (1986). *Abnormal psychology.* New York: John Wiley & Sons.

Therapist Surname and the Presenting Problems of Psychotherapy Patients: Implications for Treatment and Therapy Outcome

Ernst von Krankman, Ph.D.

The keen clinician is sensitive to the reality that the psychotherapy patient reacts subjectively to every aspect of the therapeutic situation—to the therapist's physical appearance, to the manner in which the therapist first greets the patient, and even to the way in which the therapy room is decorated. However, few therapists realize that the therapist's surname itself may elicit a strong subjective emotional reaction from the patient that may affect the ultimate course of therapy and that the magnitude of the patient's affective response may be a function of the patient's presenting problem.

Picture a male patient whose presenting problem is impotence. He calls and makes an appointment at a moderately priced mental health clinic, is seen for an hour-long screening interview with the clinical social worker, and at the end of the session is told that he will receive a call later in the week to set up his first therapy session. The call comes, his first therapy session is scheduled, and he is told that he has not yet been assigned a specific therapist, but that by the time he arrives for his appointment, a therapist will have been assigned and that the clinic receptionist will call his name when it is time for him to meet his new doctor. He arrives 45 minutes early for his appointment and sits nervously thumbing through a magazine, trying not to make eye contact with the other patients in the waiting room while wondering what their problems might be and whether there might be any other impotence-sufferers in the room. Finally, the appointed time arrives and the clinic receptionist announces to the patient, "Dr. Pecker will see you now!"

Or take the case of the college freshman who suffers from a stuttering problem and is referred by the college counselor to a walk-in clinic. After a long wait, the clinic receptionist finally announces, "Dr. Doctor will see you now."

Or the depressed patient who is referred to Dr. Downs.

Unlikely occurrences? Not really. In fact, the author is personally acquainted with psychologists with the aforementioned surnames. And it is likely that Dr. Pecker has seen patients suffering from impotence, just as it is likely that Dr. Doctor has seen patients suffering from stuttering. And given the high incidence of depression in our population, it is an almost certainty that Dr. Downs has worked with patients suffering from depression.

Predicting what subjective emotional response(s) of the patient will be elicited by any given therapist's surname is quite complex. For instance, in the majority of cases it could be predicted that patients suffering from impotence might feel ill-at-ease when confronted with a therapist named Dr. Pecker. The prognosis for successful treatment of the impotent patient, then, would not be good if the patient were to feel uncomfortable about the therapist from the very start of treatment. Of course, it is conceivable that some impotent patients might react differently, feeling relieved, if not indeed fortunate, that they have hooked up with a mental health professional who may be well-versed in their organ-specific problem. (Whether or not Dr. Pecker actually *is* well-versed in the problems of those suffering from impotence is irrelevant, since we are not dealing with objective reality, rather with the patient's subjective emotional responses, feelings, fantasies, etc.) Assuming, however, that most impotent patients would feel uncomfortable seeing a therapist with the name Dr. Pecker, we could say that this surname is by and large contraindicated (or —).

Sometimes, a therapist's surname may be indicated (or +). For example, a depressed patient may feel quite good about entering therapy with a therapist named Dr. Allbright.

And then, there are those really tough diagnostic judgment calls, when it is unclear whether a therapist's surname may be indicated or contraindicated. For instance, when confronted with a therapist named Dr. Allbright, a manic patient may feel quite positively disposed to entering treatment. Whether encouraging a manic patient to be in treatment with Dr. Allbright is therapeutic or not is uncertain. It may be that the manic would be better served by being in therapy with Dr. Downs (or better yet, Dr. Balance). We could say, here, that the wisdom of the manic patient seeing Dr. Allbright is questionable (or ?).

What other therapist surnames may be indicated or contraindicated in working with patients of various diagnostic presenting problems? In order to answer this question, the author performed an exhaustive, not to mention exhausting, search of the official Membership Register of the American Psychological Association (1987). The resultant data are presented below.

Therapist's name	Indication	Diagnostic presenting problem
Dr. Agin (particularly when seen with a co-therapist also named Dr. Agin)	—	Obsessive-compulsives
Dr. Alter	?	Transsexuals
	?	Religious patients
Dr. Angelica also Dr. Angell	—	Satan worshippers
Dr. Anon	—	Premature ejaculators
	+	Nuns who like puns
Dr. Baba	—	Stutterers
Dr. Babl	?	Autistics
Dr. Baer also Dr. Bayer	+	Headache sufferers
Dr. Balance	+	Manic-depressives
	?	Patients with a history of difficulty paying their bills
Dr. Baron also Dr. Barron	?	Patients suffering from grandiosity
Dr. Barr	?	Alcoholics
Dr. Batchelor	?	Male patients with intimacy and commitment problems
Dr. Batman	?	Patients with overactive fantasy lives
Dr. Belcher	?	Patients with gastrointestinal disorders
Dr. Bender	?	Alcoholics
Dr. Berkowitz	?	Paranoid schizophrenics suffering from command hallucinations instructing them to "Kill!"

Therapist's name	Indication	Diagnostic presenting problem
Dr. Berns *also* Dr. Burns	?	Fire setters
Dr. Best	? ?	Perfectionistic patients Anorectics
Dr. Betts *also* Dr. Betz	?	Gambling addicts
Dr. Biggerstaff *also* Dr. Biggs	—	Patients concerned with penis size
Dr. Bitter *also* Dr. Bitterman	?	Borderline personality disorders
Dr. Black *also* Dr. Blackman *also* Dr. Blackmore	—	Depressives
Dr. Blank	? ? ? ? ?	Amnesiacs Hysterics Patients suffering from "blocking" Schizoids Elective mutes
Dr. Blood	? ?	Actively psychotic patients Explosive personality disorders
Dr. Blue	—	*See* Dr. Black
Dr. Bolt	—	Patients who have had negative experiences with ECT
Dr. Bond	?	Patients with separation-individuation problems
Dr. Boot	? ? ?	Shoe fetishists Sadists Masochists
Dr. Booz	?	Alcoholics
Dr. Boring	?	Patients suffering existential dilemmas
Dr. Borow	?	Gambling addicts
Dr. Boy	?	Gender identity disorders
Dr. Braine *also* Dr. Breit	?	Patients with superiority complexes
also Dr. Breiter *also* Dr. Breitman *also* Dr. Bright *also* Dr. De Witt *also* Dr. Fulbright	?	Patients with inferiority complexes
Dr. Breed *also* Dr. Breedlove	—	Impotent patients.

Therapist's name	Indication	Diagnostic presenting problem
Dr. Brew *also* Dr. Brewer	?	Alcoholics
Dr. Brief	—	Premature ejaculators
Dr. Brimm *also* Dr. Rimm when performing co- therapy with Dr. Brimm	?	Caffeine addicts (coffee)
Dr. Broad	—	Feminist patients
Dr. Bruce	—	Patients suffering from homosexual panic
Dr. Bunshaft	—	Patients suffering from homosexual panic
Dr. Butt	? —	Nicotine addicts Patients suffering from homosexual panic
Dr. Buys	?	Compulsive shoppers
Dr. Caesar	—	Schizophrenics
Dr. Cave *also* Dr. Marsh	?	Therapists-in-training at psychoanalytic training institutes
Dr. Chance	?	Gambling addicts
Dr. Chew *also* Dr. Chu	?	Oral-aggressive and oral-sadistic patients
Dr. Church	?	Religious patients
Dr. Clapp	?	Patients with transmittable sexual diseases
Dr. Cling *also* Dr. Kling	?	Dependent personality disorders
Dr. Coke *also* Dr. Coker	?	Cocaine addicts
Dr. Comfort	+	Just about any patient
Dr. Conboy	?	Sociopaths
Dr. Copes	?	Patients with poor frustration tolerance
Dr. Couch	+	Psychoanalytic patients
Dr. Counts	?	Obsessive-compulsives
Dr. Cox	?	Female patients with penis envy
Dr. Crook	—	Just about any patient with an intact superego
	?	Sociopaths

Therapist's name	Indication	Diagnostic presenting problem
Dr. Cross	?	Religious patients
	?	Schizophrenics
Dr. Cummings	?	Premature ejaculators
	?	Impotent patients
Dr. Danish	?	Caffeine addicts (coffee)
Dr. Dear	?	Patients with intimacy problems
Dr. Dee	—	Neurologically impaired patients unable to remember even a single letter of the alphabet
Dr. Disney	?	Patients with overactive fantasy lives
Dr. Downer	—	Depressives
Dr. Dunn	—	Premature ejaculators
Dr. Elfant	—	Learning-disabled patients who have difficulty spelling "elephant"
Dr. Ends	—	Patients with suicidal ideation
	—	Patients with homosexual panic
Dr. Enter	?	Agoraphobics
Dr. Falsey	?	Female patients obsessed with breast size
Dr. Fear	—	Generalized anxiety disorders
Dr. Fee	?	Patients with difficulties paying bills
Dr. Fitts	—	Hysteric convulsives
Dr. Foreman	?	Male patients with multiple personalities ($N = 4$)
Dr. Free	+	Patients seen at municipal clinics
Dr. Friendly	?	Female hysterics
Dr. From	?	Patients obsessed with Abbott & Costello routines, e.g., "Who's on First?"
Dr. Fry	—	Floridian prison inmate patients on death row
Dr. Fuchs	?	Acting-out, antisocial, conduct-disordered, oppositional, learning-disabled, adolescent patients who encounter difficulty correctly spelling "the F word"
Dr. Fuhrer	?	Authoritarian personality disorders

Therapist's name	Indication	Diagnostic presenting problem
Dr. Funk	—	Depressives
Dr. Gamble	?	Gambling addicts
Dr. Gee	—	See Dr. Dee
Dr. Gerber	?	Regressed patients
Dr. Getoff	—	Premature ejaculators
Dr. Gigl	?	Hebephrenic schizophrenics
Dr. Glad	+	Depressives
	?	Manics
Dr. Goodwin	?	Gambling addicts
Dr. Graves	—	Patients with suicidal ideation
	?	Necrophiliacs
Dr. Hardee	—	Impotent patients
also Dr. Harden		
also Dr. Harder		
also Dr. Hardwick		
also Dr. Hardy		
Dr. Harm	—	Generalized anxiety disorders
also Dr. Harmer		
also Dr. Harms		
Dr. Hayman	?	Oppositional adolescent patients
also Dr. Hey		acting inappropriately toward
also Dr. Heyman		doctors
Dr. Heads	?	Multiple personality disorders
Dr. Heard	—	Paranoid personality disorders
	—	Paranoid schizophrenics
Dr. Hershey	?	Bulimics
	?	Anorectics
Dr. Hooker	?	Male psychosexual dysfunctions
also Dr. Horlick		
also Dr. Huneycutt		
also Dr. Hunsucker		
Dr. Howe	?	See Dr. From
Dr. Hurt	?	Masochists
	?	Sadists
Dr. Into	?	See Dr. From
Dr. Jester	?	Manics
also Dr. Jolly	+	Depressives
also Dr. Joy		
Dr. Judge	—	Guilt-ridden patients
also Dr. Justice	?	Perfectionistic patients

Therapist's name	Indication	Diagnostic presenting problem
Dr. Jury	—	*See* Dr. Judge
Dr. Kafka	?	Paranoid patients
Dr. Kaiser	—	*See* Dr. Caesar
Dr. Kidder	?	*See* Dr. Jester
Dr. Kitchen	?	Bulimics
	?	Anorectics
Dr. Klappersack	—	Patients with transmittable sexual diseases
Dr. Kluttz	?	Accident-prone and self-destructive patients
	?	Patients with poor motor control
Dr. Knapp	—	Narcoleptics
Dr. Knight	—	Patients with overactive fantasy lives
Dr. Knill	?	Nihilitistic patients
	—	Patients suffering from existential dilemmas
Dr. Krash	?	Acting-out alcoholics charged with DWI after car accidents
Dr. Krock	—	Oppositional adolescent patients
Dr. LaBier	?	Alcoholics
Dr. La Du *also* Dr. La Due	—	Encopretic children
Dr. Langstaff	—	Patients concerned with penis size
Dr. Lanktree	—	Impotent patients
Dr. Law	?	Sociopaths
Dr. Lax	+	Generalized anxiety disorders
	—	Impotent patients
Dr. Lay *also* Dr. Ley	?	Nymphomaniacs
Dr. Leary *also* Dr. Leer	—	Paranoid personality disorders
	—	Paranoid schizophrenics
Dr. Leek	?	Enuretics
Dr. Leen *also* Dr. Leight *also* Dr. Leiter *also* Dr. Leitman *also* Dr. Light *also* Dr. Lighter	? ?	Anorectics Bulimics
Dr. Lennon	—	*See* Dr. Caesar

Therapist's name	Indication	Diagnostic presenting problem
Dr. Lerner	?	Learning-disabled patients
Dr. Liberty	?	Patients suffering from existential dilemmas
	?	Prison patients
	?	Patients with bondage/dominance rituals
Dr. Lie	?	Sociopaths
also Dr. Lion	—	Paranoid personality disorders
	—	Just about all other patients
	?	Learning-disabled sociopaths who read "Lion" as "Lying"
Dr. Lilly	?	Necrophiliacs
Dr. Lincoln	—	See Dr. Caesar
Dr. Lindberg	?	Patients with fear of flying
Dr. Lips	—	Patients with tardive dyskinesia
Dr. Lipton	?	Caffeine addicts (tea)
Dr. List	?	Obsessive-compulsives
Dr. Lit	?	Fire setters
also Dr. Litt		
Dr. Lo	—	Depressives
also Dr. Loe	—	Patients with low self-esteem
also Dr. Low		
also Dr. Lowe		
Dr. Long	—	Patients concerned with penis size
also Dr. Longfellow		
Dr. Look	—	Paranoid personality disorders
	—	Paranoid schizophrenics
	?	Voyeurs
Dr. Looney	—	All patients
Dr. Lord	—	See Dr. Caesar
Dr. Love	?	Narcissistic personality disorders
Dr. Lovejoy	?	Nymphomaniacs
Dr. Luster	?	Pedophilists
Dr. Luther	—	See Dr. Caesar
Dr. Ma	?	Patients with unresolved separation-individuation problems
Dr. Macqueen	—	Patients with homosexual panic
Dr. Madden	?	Explosive personality disorders
Dr. Madonna	—	See Dr. Caesar
Dr. Maffia	?	Sociopaths

Therapist's name	Indication	Diagnostic presenting problem
Dr. Mallinger	?	Neurasthenics
Dr. Manson	?	Paranoid schizophrenics
Dr. Maze	—	Cognitively confused patients
	—	Neurologically impaired patients
Dr. Meaney	?	Sadists
also Dr. Meany	?	Masochists
	—	Young children entering therapy
Dr. Mechanic	?	Schizoids
Dr. Meek	?	Patients lacking assertiveness skills
Dr. Milestone	?	Patients in midlife crises
Dr. Monday	—	Depressives
Dr. Monk	?	Avoidant personality disorders
Dr. Moody	?	Manic-depressives
Dr. Moreland	?	Agoraphobics
Dr. Moses	—	See Dr. Caesar
Dr. Nero	?	Fire setters
Dr. Numbers	—	Learning-disabled patients with poor arithmetic skills
	?	Obsessive-compulsives
Dr. Nutt	—	All patients
Dr. O'Rear	?	Patients with homosexual panic
Dr. Organ	?	Patients with psychosomatic complaints
Dr. Orr	?	See Dr. From
Dr. Overcash	?	Compulsive shoppers
Dr. Overcast	—	Depressives
Dr. Overlade	?	Nymphomaniacs
	?	Patients with sexual preoccupations
Dr. Overton	—	Anorectics
	—	Bulimics
Dr. Pabst	?	Alcoholics
Dr. Pain	?	Masochists
also Dr. Payne	?	Sadists
	—	All other patients
Dr. Pall	—	Depressives
Dr. Paradise	?	Patients with overactive fantasy lives
	+	All other patients

Therapist's name	Indication	Diagnostic presenting problem
Dr. Parent	?	Child and adolescent patients
Dr. Parrott	?	Stutterers
	?	Obsessive-compulsives
Dr. Peak	?	Voyeurs
Dr. Peel	?	Exhibitionists
also Dr. Peele	?	Voyeurs
Dr. Pennypacker	−	Patients concerned with penis size
Dr. Pepper	−	Anorectics
	−	Bulimics
Dr. Peter	?	Male psychosexual dysfunctions
also Dr. Peters		
Dr. Polite	?	Explosive personality disorders
Dr. Pope	−	*See* Dr. Caesar
Dr. Popoff	−	Premature ejaculators
also Dr. Popper		
Dr. Query	−	Paranoid personality disorders
	−	Paranoid schizophrenics
Dr. Quick	−	Premature ejaculators
	−	Depressed patients with psychomotor retardation
	−	Learning-disabled patients
	−	Patients with IQs below 80
Dr. Quittmann	−	Underachievers
	−	Patients with poor frustration tolerance
Dr. Ragland	?	Female patients suffering from intense PMS
Dr. Rambo	?	Explosive personality disorders
	?	Unassertive patients
Dr. Rampage	?	Explosive personality disorders
	?	Paranoid schizophrenics
Dr. Rapp	+	Musically inclined minority patients
Dr. Read	?	Dyslexics
also Dr. Reading		
also Dr. Redmore		
also Dr. Ried		
Dr. Reagan	−	Homeless patients
Dr. Reams	−	Patients suffering from homosexual panic
also Dr. Reardon		
also Dr. Reback		

Therapist's name	Indication	Diagnostic presenting problem
Dr. Record	—	Paranoid personality disorders
	—	Paranoid schizophrenics
	—	Learning-disabled patients having difficulty reading such words as "wind," "invalid," "minute," and "polish"
Dr. Redwine	?	Alcoholics
Dr. Reiter	—	Dysgraphics
Dr. Riel	?	Patients encountering difficulties with reality testing
Dr. Risk	?	Gambling addicts
Dr. Roundy	—	Anorectics
	—	Bulimics
Dr. Royalty	?	Patients suffering from writer's block
Dr. Rude	?	Narcissistic personality disorders
	?	Sociopaths
	?	Oppositional disorders
Dr. Ruff *also* Dr. Ruffman	?	Sadists
	?	Masochists
Dr. Rule *also* Dr. Rutman	?	Obsessive-compulsives
Dr. Rust	?	Patients suffering from senile dementia
Dr. Saad	?	Depressives with marked psychomotor retardation
	?	Depressed, learning-disabled patients with spelling difficulties
Dr. St. Peter	—	*See* Dr. Caesar
Dr. Sale	?	Compulsive shoppers
Dr. Samson	?	Patients with inferiority complexes
	?	Neurasthenics
Dr. Sandman	+	Patients with sleep disturbances
Dr. Savage	?	Sadists
	?	Masochists
Dr. Scholl	?	Foot fetishists
Dr. Schooler	?	Truant school-age children entering therapy

Therapist's name	Indication	Diagnostic presenting problem
Dr. Search	?	Patients with existential dilemmas
Dr. Self	?	Schizophrenics
	?	Personality disorders
Dr. Severance	—	Patients with castration anxieties
Dr. Shields	?	Defensive patients
	?	Female patients with heavy menstrual flow
Dr. Shine	+	Depressives
	?	Manics
Dr. Shoemaker	?	Foot fetishists
Dr. Shows	?	Narcissistic personality disorders
	?	Exhibitionists
Dr. Sixty	+	Patients age 60 and younger
	—	Patients over 60
Dr. Slaughter	?	Sadists
	?	Masochists
	—	All other patients
Dr. Son	—	Patients older than the therapist
Dr. Sparks	?	Manics
Dr. Speck	—	Obsessive-compulsives with cleaning rituals
Dr. Speisman also Dr. Spyer	—	Paranoid personality disorders
	—	Paranoid schizophrenics
Dr. Spellman	—	Paranoid patients who believe that their thinking is being controlled by others
Dr. Spotts	—	See Dr. Speck
Dr. Stern also Dr. Stickler	?	Patients with strict upbringings
Dr. Stix	?	Anorectics
Dr. Stout	—	Anorectics
	—	Bulimics
Dr. Strange	—	Just about all patients
Dr. Super	?	Patients with inferiority complexes
	?	Patients with superiority complexes
	+	California patients
Dr. Swan	—	Patients with poor self-esteem involving their looks

Therapist's name	Indication	Diagnostic presenting problem
Dr. Swift	—	Premature ejaculators
Dr. Test also Dr. Tester	—	Patients with test anxiety
Dr. Toogood	?	Perfectionists
Dr. Troll	—	Patients having difficulties with reality testing
	?	Alcoholics with delirium tremens
Dr. True	?	Compulsive liars
also Dr. Trueman	?	Sociopaths
Dr. Udick	—	Paranoid male patients who project concerns about their sexual organ onto others
Dr. Vane	?	Narcissistic personality disorders
Dr. Vice	?	Patients with overpunitive superegos
Dr. Wagstaff	?	Patients concerned with penis size
Dr. Wanderer also Dr. Wandersman	?	Patients experiencing difficulty with commitment
Dr. Warholic	?	Explosive personality disorders
also Dr. Warman	?	Aggressive patients
Dr. Warner	?	Generalized anxiety disorders
Dr. Watchman	?	Paranoid personality disorders
	?	Paranoid schizophrenics
	?	TV addicts
	?	Voyeurs
Dr. Watt	+	Patients suffering from seasonal affective disorders
Dr. Waxman	—	Catatonic schizophrenics
Dr. Waybright	+	Depressives
	?	Manics
	?	Patients with IQs below 70 (mentally retarded)
Dr. Weary	—	Depressives
	—	Neurasthenics
Dr. Wedding	?	Unmarried patients experiencing difficulty committing to their partners
Dr. Well also Dr. Wellman	+	Just about all patients
Dr. Wetter	?	Enuretics

Therapist's name	Indication	Diagnostic presenting problem
Dr. Wild *also* Dr. Wildman	?	Borderline personality disorders
Dr. Wills	—	Depressive patients with suicidal ideation
Dr. Win *also* Dr. Winborn *also* Dr. Winner *also* Dr. Wynne	?	Gambling addicts
Dr. Wine *also* Dr. Winer *also* Dr. Winogrond	?	Alcoholics
Dr. Work *also* Dr. Workie *also* Dr. Workman	?	Workaholics
Dr. Worth	+	Patients with low self-esteem
Dr. Wyspianski	—	Learning-disabled patients
Dr. Young *also* Dr. Youngblood *also* Dr. Youth	?	Patients with midlife crises
Dr. Zaza	—	Stutterers

Future Directions

The author has identified hundreds of therapist surnames, drawn from the official roster of the American Psychological Association, that may be indicated or contraindicated in the treatment of psychotherapy patients. Because of space and time limitations, this paper is necessarily limited to the investigation of surnames of psychologists. Had the official directories of the other mental health professions (e.g., psychiatry, social work, etc.) been investigated, it is likely that hundreds more equally relevant surnames would have been identified. The author leaves such related investigation to future studies.

Another area deserving of investigation involves the relationship between *patient's surname* and therapist's subjective emotional response. For example, picture a therapist meeting a patient for the first time, only to discover that the patient's surname is Sue (or some identical-sounding surname, such as Sioux, Soo, or Sew). The therapist's feelings elicited by the patient's surname may affect the course of treatment and hence the therapy outcome if, for instance, the therapist has reservations about working with a potentially litigious patient. It is the author's sincere hope that the constantly probing researchers who epitomize the scientifically based field of clinical psychology will pursue this vital avenue of research further by undertaking to identify key surnames of potential patients, thereby insuring that clinicians will at least be aware of the possibilities of positive and negative affective reactions of therapists to patients' surnames. Perhaps these dedicated researchers could begin the monumental task of identifying key surnames of potential patients by studying that great mass of raw data that just sits awaiting assessment—the 1,709 pages of the Manhattan telephone directory (New York Telephone, 1988).

References

American Psychological Association. (1987). *1987 APA membership register.* Washington, DC: Author.

New York Telephone. (1988). *NYNEX white pages (Manhattan).* New York: NYNEX Information Resources Company.

How to Be an Ericksonian (Milton, Not Erik)

Linda Chamberlain, M.S.
University of Denver

What psychotherapist has not dreamt of having been a part of that fledgling group that studied with Freud in Vienna, Rogers (Carl, not Mr.) in Wisconsin, or Skinner at Harvard. Well, it's too late for that. Their disciples have already been chosen and sent out into the academic and professional world to spread their testaments. Although few people actually get to work beside the great theorists in our field, many more of us can get in on the publicity and profits that follow shortly after the select few begin to set up their own groups of followers. Witness the phenomena of the neo-Freudians, the post-neo-Freudians, the neo-post-neo-Freudians, the pseudo-post-neo-Freudians, etc. It is the intent of this article to alert professionals to a recent major theorist who is assuredly soon to be highly influential in the psychological community. Milton H. Erickson is fast becoming legendary and now is the time to become associated with his work if you want to have the opportunity to publish lots of articles and books (particularly thick and costly ones) and make the profitable lecture circuit.

Becoming an Ericksonian therapist is no easy task. Milton Erickson's theories and techniques are often incredibly obtuse and abstract and, since he rarely wrote anything himself, his work is open to varied interpretation by those insiders who form the core of his followers. And interpret they have. Many current Ericksonians have been forced to create separate rooms in their homes or offices just to contain the volumes of work about Erickson, most of which have seductive titles like *I Talked to Erickson Personally Myself* (Plankton, 1971) and "What Milton Said Indirectly to Me" (Rossini, 1979). To save others the superhuman effort of trying to grasp what Erickson was attempting to express, I have outlined the necessary and sufficient ideas and information that one should display in order to be identified as an "Ericksonian."

Principle #1: Wear Lots of Purple

All good Ericksonians know that it was Milton's favorite color because he was reportedly color-blind except for purple. (Also, all legitimate books on Erickson are bound in purple.)

Principle #2: Know One or Two Good Metaphors

These are not your basic simple little sayings like "All the world's a stage." These are long, involved stories that are reported to make some absolutely astounding "unconscious changes." There are approximately 3.4 million of these in the books about Erickson and if you are associating with other Ericksonians, you had better know a few metaphors or at least be able to recognize one when you hear it. An example from Rossini (1979) is: "So one-a day God calls the Pope and says, 'Hey Pope, I got-a some good news, I got-a some bad news.' And the Pope says, 'So what's the good news?' and God says, 'From now on, there will be just one religion, all people united.' And the Pope says, 'That's-a great; so what's the bad news?' and God says, 'I'm-a calling from Salt Lake City.'" This is a good basic metaphor, but they need not have a punch line or even make sense. Any long, complex story that involves lots of symbolism is adequate for beginners.

Principle #3: Make Simple, Enlightened Statements about Erickson's Work

Be able to emphatically state "He wasn't just a hypnotist" or "He wasn't just a psychotherapist" in opposition to what the other Ericksonians in your group are saying. You don't have to do anything else—they will take it from there.

Principle #4: Know How to Really *Use* "Inductions"

When a group of Ericksonians are talking about inductions, do not make the mistake of thinking they are about going into the military. This has to do with all that hypnotic stuff that Milton was always doing, the main focus of which seemed to be to get people to close their eyes without saying "Close your eyes." In fact, if you really want to impress an Ericksonian, wait until someone in the group gets bored enough to become sleepy and close his/her eyes. Then take credit for having done an induction without anyone becoming aware of what you were doing while the conversation was going on (Ziegfried, 1984).

Principle #5: Go to Phoenix, Arizona

Plan a pilgrimage to Phoenix for your next vacation. Visit the Erickson home, the Erickson family, the Erickson Foundation, and plan to climb Squaw Peak (at dawn) as that is reportedly where Milton's ashes are scattered. It is even better if you can plan this during an International Congress on Ericksonian Approaches to Hypnosis and Psychotherapy that is held every few years for the clan to gather and compare notes. This is where you are sure to find lots of the inner circle of Ericksonians. Be sure to wear lots of purple.

Principle #6: Know How to Use the "Confusion Technique"

If you make a serious faux pas when saying something about Erickson and find that the conversation comes to a screeching halt and all eyes are narrowly turned on you, simply comment how you have been working on that comment as a specific use of "trance induction through the confusion technique." Beware of resorting to this, however, as you may then be elected president of your local

Erickson Institute or be asked to review and edit some Erickson monographs.

Principle #7: Have a Significant, Meaningful Experience Caused by Erickson

Try to associate yourself with Erickson as directly as possible (keep in mind that he died in 1980 so you could not have had too direct a contact with him after that). However, if you are desperate and want to go all out, you can report that something you saw on one of Erickson's videotapes planted an image of him in your unconscious mind and that now when you go into trance, you see him and hear his voice. Relate as many personal anecdotes (these are even better than the metaphors already mentioned) about how Erickson said or wrote something that changed your life. You might try: "After watching a film of Milton working with an anorectic teenage girl, I found I could remember all the words to 'Louie, Louie'" (Fershur, 1981) or "About a month after I read his induction with the paraplegic, blind, Portuguese dwarf, hair started to grow over my bald spot" (Haley, 1984).

Principle #8: Know Your Ericksonian Vocabulary

In conversations with Ericksonians, it is important to be able to respond to key words that are vital to Erickson's work but ambiguous enough that you can use them relatively freely without anyone being the wiser (those who are Freudians should already be adept at this). Try to use these words and phrases as much as possible: indirect, unconscious (not used in relation to drinking too much at the APA Happy Hour), metaphor, trance, induction, implied directives, utilization, indirect associative focusing, ideocognitive processes, multiple levels of communication, intercontextual cues, depotentiating conscious mental sets, catalepsy, pulsation changes, phenomenological experience as state-bound learning, the non sequitur double bind, posthypnotic suggestion, negative hallucinations, and spontaneous trance phenomena. For those of you who wish to become truly competent, my *Dictionary of Ericksonian Words and*

Phrases (Chamberlain, in press) will soon be available and is guaranteed to help you sound like Milton himself in just a few days (if you order early, only $69.99!).

References

Chamberlain, L. (in press). *Dictionary of Ericksonian Words and Phrases.* Denver: Chamberlain Books/Fast Bucks Press.

Fershur, Kimberly. (1981). I was a teenage Ericksonian. *Psychoteen Magazine, 22,* 112–113.

Haley, Bubba J. (1984). So O.K., who is this guy anyway? In J. B. Haley (Ed.), *The power tactics of Sylvester Stallone.* Jersey City, NJ: Read Dis Book.

Plankton, S. (1971). *I talked to Erickson personally myself.* Phoenix: Indirect Press.

Rossini, Ernesto. (1979). What Milton said indirectly to me. In E. Rossini (Ed.), *I'm-a an Ericksonian and you're-a not.* Rome: Psychologhetti Pressa.

Ziegfried, Jeffrey. (1984). What he really said he meant to say he was saying is what he said to me once. *Clarification Monthly, 10,* 300–599.

Beyond Therapeutic Neutrality: Cure by Negation

Eric D. Lister, M.D.
Exeter Mental Health Associates

Freud's adage that the therapist should remain neutral in the face of a patient's intrapsychic conflict has been a guiding principle long-accepted by psychoanalysts and psychoanalytic psychotherapists alike. Nevertheless, the practice of inpatient psychiatry has led this author to appreciate the fundamentally curative forces which follow from *actively opposing* the patient's every desire. The "science" of dialectics might well have suggested, decades ago, that there would *have* to be some antithesis required by the "thesis" of neutrality (for it would be impossibly simple to assume that neutrality itself represents the synthesis of positive and negative reactions to the patient). Therapeutic obstructionism is the true antithesis to neutrality.

Applications

Therapeutic obstructionism can be seen as the cornerstone of successful inpatient treatment, from preadmission interview through discharge. The following examples illustrate the beauty of this innovative therapeutic paradigm.

If patients want to be admitted to the hospital, we say that they cannot and present them with a list of preadmission demands stopping just short of the impossible.

If patients do not want to be admitted to the hospital, we either tell them that they cannot be admitted, even if they wanted to, or that they have to be admitted.

If patients in the hospital want passes to spend time outside the hospital, we suggest that they are trying to escape from the intensity of the therapeutic work.

If patients want to stay in the hospital and do not ask for passes, we suggest that they are trying to escape from the requirement that they practice out in the real world what they are learning in the hospital.

If patients do not want medication, we insist that this is a requirement of treatment and that their resistance is a reflection of paranoia.

If patients want medication, we express our concern that they might be looking to magical chemicals to do what really needs to be done through psychological exploration and hard work.

When patients spend time alone, we tell them that they should be with other people.

When patients spend time with other people, we wonder if they might not need to spend more time alone.

When patients with eating disorders want to go to the bathroom, we lock the door.

When other patients refuse to go to the bathroom, we encourage the use of laxatives.

Patients who want to sleep late are told to get up early; those who want to get up early are encouraged to sleep and get their rest.

Patients who do not want to participate in groups are told that precisely those groups which they wish to avoid are the groups central to their treatment programs, and those who ask to participate in every group are encouraged to spend more time outside of the hospital.

Patients who want to leave the hospital are told that they need to stay; those who want to stay in the hospital are told they need a date for discharge.

Patients who are quick to say goodbye are encouraged to stay a little longer; those who resist saying goodbye are pressed with an ever-approaching discharge date.

Successful Treatment: A Case Study

A 26-year-old teacher, whose interpersonal problems had been long-standing, was told by his wife that unless he got help she would leave him. Under this pressure, he asked to be admitted to the hospital.

Following the principles of obstructionism, hospitalization was re-fused, and the patient told that he was inadequately motivated for treatment. His wife then threw him out of their home, at which point he raised such a ruckus that the police were called and he was brought to the emergency room in their custody. At that point, he was told that he would have to stay in the hospital, regardless of his vociferous objections, and that the only alternative was commitment to a state institution.

Upon admission to the hospital, the patient wanted to talk about nothing but his problems at home and his sense of outrage at his wife. Therefore, our treatment plan focused exclusively upon diffi-culties with people at other times in his life. The patient refused family therapy, at which point we let him know as gently as possible that any increase in privileges would be contingent upon his accep-tance of family therapy. When he was confronted by other patients in therapy groups, he decided that the groups were useless and he refused to participate further. At that point, we told the patient that he would be discharged. He objected, saying that he had no place to go. We therefore insisted that he participate in all therapy groups and, in fact, added extra groups to his treatment program as a requirement for continued hospitalization.

In the context of our tenacious adherence to the principles enumerated above, the patient and his wife planned a reconciliation, his siblings and employer rallied behind him and stated that he had never seemed so reasonable or thoughtful in his life, and the patient asked to be discharged. We, of course, refused, but in a spirit of compromise agreed to discharge him 1 week later. A 6-month fol-low-up after discharge reveals that the patient's marriage and pro-fessional life remain stable and that there have been no other epi-sodes of major distress.

Discussion and Conclusion

Independent researchers, long ago departed from the orthodoxy of psychoanalysis, have described related techniques as "paradox" and "counterparadox" without fully realizing the momentous nature of their innovations. It is with a sense of awe (that natural laws can be so symmetrical, so perfect) that the author must delineate the limits of the theory of obstructionism.

Thus far, the reader who appreciates fully the deep meaning and universal applicability of this theory must inevitably be thinking of the countless ways in which theory can be translated into technique, with resulting benefit to all mankind. It is precisely at this point where we inevitably discover the limits of the theory, namely, that it dictates that we must not only oppose the patient's every expressed desire, but that we must *also* oppose our own desire to utilize this theory. That is, whenever a therapist feels inclined to act oppositionally, guided by these precepts, he/she must be prepared to *oppose his/her own technique* and respond precisely in the way requested by the patient, a technique known as "counteroppositionism."

In conclusion, the practice of this psychotherapeutic technique is quite taxing, requiring as it does of the therapist not only the capacity for negation and self-negation, but also a willingness to reject these negations! Hallowed though our psychological forefathers may be, their overzealous embrace of the principles of neutrality may have been, in fact, a countertransferential avoidance of the excruciating responsibility which necessarily follows when one adopts the theory and practice of oppositionism and counteroppositionism and attempts to master the unbroken thread of self-knowledge necessary for practicing on such a rigorous level.

2
Psychoanalysis

Psychoanalysis: A Layperson's Guide to Theory and Technique

Carolyn Murphy, M.A.
University of Maryland

Psychoanalytic literature can be rather ponderous for the novice reader unfamiliar with the basic concepts. The purpose of the present paper is to simply and clearly outline the key elements of psychoanalysis so that even a layperson can understand this powerful and robust theory and technique.

Psychoanalytic theory postulates that psychological problems begin at a very young age. Indeed, many patients' deficits are rooted in an early lack of healthy "object relations." Object relations theories are derived from the supposition that "objects who need objects are the luckiest objects in the world" (Streisand, 1967, line 1).

Analytic theory also maintains that many, most, and/or all psychological problems are linked to sexual organs and sexual functioning. Indeed, modern psychoanalytic theorists are only beginning to appreciate fully Freud's insight that the penis itself is a necessary and sufficient condition for therapeutic change.

Unlike therapists of other theoretical persuasions, psychoanalysts have a variety of powerful techniques at their disposal to effect change and bring about successful therapeutic outcome. Among some of these techniques are "confrontation" (making key issues evident to the patient), "clarification" (focusing on issues), "interpretation" (making the unconscious conscious), and "working through." For those readers unfamiliar with "working through," a precise definition is currently being worked through.

No outline of psychoanalytic concepts would be complete without a clinical case to spice up the presentation. The case to be presented is that of a 27-year-old male, unable to achieve satisfaction, although he tried (Jagger & Richards, 1965). In this lively patient-therapist interaction, which takes place during the 86th session of treatment, we see a fine example of an effective "interpretation."

Patient: I don't know—I just seem to feel really low sometimes.

Analyst: Your borderline incestuous yearnings for your maternal figure began preverbally, when your libidinally eroticized fantasies were at their peak. There is a primitive, primarily processed regression which, I hate to tell you, is in no way in the service of your fragile ego. Your impulse-ridden "self" has clearly been injured in a quasi-narcissistic fashion, causing an ego-syntonic negative transference, which is manifested in your homosexual longings for me.

Patient: Wow! Could you repeat that! Does this mean I'm cured?

Dealing with transference issues is also critical in psychoanalysis. Nothing is quite as powerful as an interpretation of the transference. Take, for example, this revealing interchange in the 9,832nd session (during the "working through" period).

Patient: I'm really getting interested in this woman that lives next door to me. I feel very attracted to her.

Analyst: Mmm hmm. And could it be that this attraction is connected to my sexual longings for you? I mean, your sexual longings for me?

Patient: Was that what they call a Freudian slip?

Analyst: I'm sorry, our time is up for today.

Dreams are an important tool used to pave the road to the patient's unconscious, especially when followed by free association.

Patient: I had this really weird dream last night. I was about 5 years old. I sneaked into my parents' bedroom and killed my father. God knows why. The next thing you know I'm in a church about to get married. I look over at my bride-to-be, and damned if it isn't my mother!

> And the whole time, I had this image of my father chasing me around with a freshly sharpened machete. Pretty weird, huh?
>
> Analyst: And what is your association to "weird"?
>
> Patient: Why, what's *your* association to "weird"?
>
> Analyst: Weird. Weirdo. Doe Ray Me. Julie Andrews. Poppins. Pop out. Of my mind? You bet. Your life. Groucho Marx. Lenin. McCartney. Liverpool. Of blood. Red. Skeleton. Scary. Wife. Headache. Barry Manilow. Armageddon. Sex. That horse. Of course. Mr. Ed. Sullivan. Harry Stack. Stacked. You know who. Incredible. Edible. Oedipal, shmedipal.
>
> Patient: I see.

Indubitably, dream interpretation is a must.

The successful psychoanalyst, early on in his/her career, learns the wisdom of Freud's taboo against gratifying patients' wishes—there's a crucial difference between what the patient wants and what the patient needs. One way to defer patient gratification is to not answer any personal questions that may be asked. Provide a response that does not reveal self-disclosing information but that instead opens the door to the patient's associations and fantasies. A good technique to use in this type of situation is prolonged silence.

> Patient: Nice day, isn't it?
>
> Analyst: (*silence*)
>
> Patient: How 'bout those Mets?
>
> Analyst: (*silence*)
>
> Patient: (*turning around on the couch*) Boo!
>
> Analyst: (*jumps back slightly*) (*silence*)
>
> Patient: Boo makes me think of boo hoo. I guess I do feel like crying.
>
> Analyst: And what is your association to "hoo"?
>
> Patient: Who?
>
> Analyst: What?

Thus, we see that the analyst's use of silence can be instrumental in facilitating appropriate insight and affect.

Finally, conducting analysis is a difficult job which can cause stress in analysts themselves. Analysts' internal reactions which are rooted in their own unresolved conflicts are termed "countertransference." Well-analyzed analysts keep their countertransferential reactions in check so as not to negatively influence the therapeutic process. It is important that analysts with extreme countertransferential reactions to patients discuss these reactions with their own analysts, who will in turn discuss their own countertransferential reactions to their analyst patients with their own analysts, who will in turn discuss their own countertransferential reactions to their analyst patient's countertransference to their analyst patient's countertransferences to their patient, who will probably become an analyst someday.

References

Jagger, Mick, & Richards, Keith. (1965). (*I can't get no*) *satisfaction* [Song]. London: RCA Records.

Streisand, Barbra. (1967). Objects. In B. Streisand, *Greatest hits: Volume I*. New York: RCA Records.

3
Psychodiagnostics

Moving Diagnoses: The Clinical Iconography of Bumper Stickers

Pasquale Accardo, M.D.,
and Barbara Y. Whitman, Ph.D.
St. Louis University Medical Center

Introduction

In his seminal report on parking by diagnosis, Schofield (1984) overlooked the more obvious utility of his nosologic topology. This deficit was remedied by Pittenger (1985) who, instead of requiring the patient to park by diagnosis, encouraged the therapist to observe the patient's spontaneous parking behavior as one of the more salient symptoms of his/her diagnosis. The purpose of the present report is to extend the diagnostic usefulness of the patient's automotive behavior to the situation in which the vehicle is still in motion. The high cost and limited accessibility of parking at major treatment centers makes such an extension of diagnostic methodology imperative. The increasing percentage of time which the American people spend in their cars should contribute to the cost effectiveness of the procedure.

Methodology and Results

There are five potentially useful vehicular observations available to the mobile diagnostician.

1. *The make, model, and condition of an automobile*, while at first of seemingly great diagnostic potential, is actually of very limited clini-

Supported in very small part by very small grants from the Division of Motor Vehicles, State Highway Patrol (Broderick Crawford Memorial Research Fund), and the Department of Transportation.

cal utility. The exceedingly high incidence with which cars are lent, borrowed, and stolen makes this indicator highly inexact if not worthless as a diagnostic marker.

2. *The manner in which a vehicle is manipulated in traffic* is highly subject to road and weather conditions, traffic patterns, and the state of repair of the vehicle's internal moving parts to such an extent that, with the rare exception of substance abuse (as is well known to various law enforcement agencies), it remains exceedingly difficult to tease out diagnostic patterns of driving styles. Even when it is possible to control all the relevant variables, the resultant observations (e.g., "She drives just like a woman,""He drives like a maniac") are exceedingly vague.

3. *"Baby on board" signs*, while offering a great variety of personalized self-revelations, present two major difficulties to the mobile diagnostician. First, they are difficult to read from safe distances. Second, they are predominantly untrue. How many cars with a yellow "baby on board" sign actually have a baby on board? Indeed, this single critical example suggests that the driver of any car with a little yellow square sign in the rear window has a presumptive diagnosis of pathological liar.

4. *Vanity license plates*, while occasionally of diagnostic utility, have a fairly limited scope. The overwhelming majority of vanity plates are family names or initials, or a repetition of the car make and model. A large proportion of the remainder are unintelligible to anyone. Research is currently sadly lacking as to whether the spelling used on many of these plates is a reflection of the limited number of letters available for the plate, the previous allocation of the logo (correctly spelled), a major deficiency in the American pedagogical system, or a much higher incidence of learning disability in the general population than previously hypothesized. All things considered, it does not seem fair to expect the patient to self-diagnose in just over a half dozen letters when the professional cannot accomplish the same in just over a half dozen syllables (it being understood that fairness has no conceivable relationship to either the diagnostic or therapeutic process). There are two final limitations on the use of vanity plates as diagnostic markers: first, they entail an additional (if not significant) fiscal expense, and, second, they reflect a permanence inconsistent with potential spontaneous remission or cure. In sum, vanity plates support a diagnosis of vanity.

5. *Bumper stickers* provide just the right balance between flexibil-

ity/availability and permanence to serve as potentially useful markers for personality disorders. They also retain their diagnostic utility when the car being driven is borrowed or stolen. Patients with a given mental disorder would sooner be dead than caught driving a car with the inappropriate bumper sticker. Consider what unusual circumstances would be necessary to force a liberal Democrat to get behind the wheel of a car with a pro-Reagan bumper sticker.[1]

For the present study the following motorized vehicles were excluded for obvious reasons: motorcycles, semis, taxicabs, busses, vanpool vans, and other publicly or commercially owned vehicles. School logos and parking stickers were also excluded, as were local boosters and license plate frames on the order of "Happiness is. . . ." Table 1 lists sample hypothesized correlations between selected bumper stickers and psychodiagnostic categories.

In the present study, 1,000 consecutive moving vehicles[2] were surveyed. Vanity plates were noted on 6.76% of all cars; one or more bumper stickers were observed on 2.79% of all cars. In a totally unexpected dichotomy it was found that there was no overlap between cars with vanity plates and cars with bumper stickers (although there was significant overlap of both categories with little yellow squares). The diagnostic significance of this observation is obviously very serious but will require more detailed investigation. The researchers were able to validate the tentative psychodiagnosis by bumper sticker (BSP) in only 17.5% of the cases when traffic allowed us to pass or pull up alongside the disturbed driver. The physiognomy was then compared with that published by Szondi (1952).[3] The resulting correlation of 0.41 was low, but if one recalls that Szondi's system of facial elective affinities was only valid for diagnostic pairs, then the true correlation is actually 0.82. A hy-

[1]There is a sixth potentially useful observation, but it is of merely antiquarian interest. Several decades ago a bobble-headed animal miniature located in the car's rear window was highly indicative of microcephalic oligophrenia on the part of the driver.

[2]The pioneering study on the significance of the parked car (I. Kinsey & U. Kinkey, *The Kama Sutra and the Drive-In: The Ecology of Popular Culture and the Topology of Sexual Positions.* St. Louis: Hoosier Press, 1979) is unfortunately much too analytical in orientation for the brief therapy bias of the present study.

[3]An updating of both the diagnostic terminology and the photodiagrams was necessary. For example, when a photo of Alan Alda was used for the gender identity confusion associated with pro-ERA bumper stickers, a higher correlation was noted for female than for male patients.

Table 1. Bumper Sticker Psychodiagnostics (BSP)

Subject/category/example	Diagnosis
"Have you hugged someone else's kid today?"	Sexual perversion, involving minors (pedophilia)
"I love my [picture of pet animal]"	Sexual perversion, involving animals (zoophilia)
"I love [city]"	Sexual perversion, involving place (geophilia)
Ecological/environmentalist	Sexual perversion, involving planet (terraphilia)
Pro-NRA	Paranoid ideation
Anti-NRA	Phobic disorder
Pro-ERA	Gender identity confusion with homo-erotic tendency
Election sticker more than 2 years old	Alzheimer's disease, early stage
Two contradictory bumper stickers	Neurotic conflict
Three or more contradictory bumper stickers	Neurotic conflict, resolving into multiple personality
Heine wine	Somatoform disorder with anal symptomatology
AM radio station	Borderline intelligence
AM stereo radio station	Mental retardation, unspecified
FM radio station	Narcissistic personality disorder
Rock radio station/rock group	Arrested adolescence with or without substance abuse disorder
Fast food chain	Bulimia
Shopping ("Born to shop," "A woman's place is in the mall")	Compulsive/addictive disorder
Bingo	Compulsive gambling
Anti-55 m.p.h. speed limit	Self-destructive tendencies
Pro-55 m.p.h. speed limit	Obsessive-compulsive disorder
Cosmetics	June Cleaver/Total Woman syndrome
"I brake for . . ."	Catatonia, sudden onset
"I'd rather be . . ."	Dissociative disorder with repression
Biblical quotations	Religiosity, rule out manic-depression and schizophrenia, paranoid type
Anti-nuclear weapons/power	Global depression
Sports	Voyeurism, sadistic subtype
Explicitly erotic ("A hard man is good to find")	Nymphomania/Don Juanism
Social extrovert ("Party animal")	Mania
Amusement park	Peter Pan syndrome
"Honk if you . . ."	Auditory hallucination
"Jews for Jesus"	Conversion disorder
"I found it"	Kleptomania

pothesis still untested would predict an even higher correlation between the respective bumper stickers on two cars involved in an automobile accident.

Conclusions and Therapeutic Implications

Bumper Stickers Psychodiagnosis (BSP) is in its infancy. The present clinical and epidemiological study documents the sensitivity of this screening method. Specificity studies are currently under way. However, if this new diagnostic technique is to have any lasting impact, it will need to have its own specific therapeutic modality. The use of car phones or CB radios for therapeutic purposes is highly unsuitable in that it still necessitates patient contact time. If the diagnostic bumper sticker has a true ontological relationship with the ongoing psychopathology, then one should be able to have significant therapeutic impact by the simple measure of superimposing on the pathological logo a new bumper sticker—"I am in therapy." The stickers should be available only from licensed therapists. Printed in a graded series to reflect the progress of the therapy, the stickers should be distributed for appropriately therapeutic fees. The present authors are not naive enough to consider this new treatment modality a mental health panacea, but they do hope that its development will represent at least one small step towards turning the insanity on America's highways to more than small therapeutic profit.

References

Pittenger, J. B. (1985). A brief report of a psychodiagnostic system for mental health clinic patients: Diagnosis by parking. *Journal of Polymorphous Perversity, 2*(2), 8.

Schofield, L. J., Jr. (1984). A brief report of a psychodiagnostic system for mental health clinic patients: Parking by diagnosis. *Journal of Polymorphous Perversity, 1*(2), 9.

Szondi, L. (1952). *Experimental diagnostics of drives* (Gertrude Aull, Trans.). New York: Grune & Stratton.

The Vicious Cycle:
The Pre-Menstrual Syndrome
(PMS) and Beyond

**Kathleen Donald, Ph.D., Ellie Kincade, M.A.,
and Robin Layman**
University of North Carolina at Asheville

Prior to the rise of the feminist movement, the notion of periodic feminine mood swings was common knowledge (Ragg, 1958). Although a well-documented phenomenon, these menstrual mood modulations were not necessarily well-received by either the women experiencing the symptoms (Kurse, Kramp, & Payne, 1960) or by those who were subjected to the interpersonal effects of these symptoms (Crabbe, 1962). With the emergence of militant feminism in the 1970s (Brauburn, 1973), the mere mention of menstrual moodiness raised eyebrows and hackles and immediately branded one, whether male or female, a male chauvinist pig (Porkas & Hogge, 1975). Seemingly overnight the period became a dead issue. Period.

Needless to say, this ultra-feminist dictate caused considerable confusion for everyone and did not hold sway for very long. Like the proverbial phoenix, the menstrual cycle was resurrected, reborn, renovated, and made relevant to the new decade of the 1980s (Tex, Ponnz, & Doosh, 1981).

The menses is now back in vogue, not only in *Vogue*, but also in *Cosmopolitan*, *The New Woman*, *Redbook*, *Good Housekeeping*, *Psychology Today*, and even *Scientific American*, to name just a few. Professional journals and popular magazines abound with articles about "the Pre-Menstrual Syndrome (PMS)." Currently riding the crest of a wave of popularity, the premenstruum, with its physiological, behavioral, and emotional concomitants, is not only recognized and discussed openly but has also attained a legitimacy and acceptance hitherto unknown. Physicians, psychologists, gynecologists, sexologists, and criminologists all have something to say about PMS (Phleaux, 1985).

Recent Developments

Past research on PMS has shown that the female PMS-sufferer generally complains of the following symptoms: irritability, combativeness, hostility, depression, anxiety, hypersensitivity, tearfulness, physical discomfort, tension, increased appetite, intellectual impairment, and lethargy. Such research, however, has been marred by the fact that no control group of non-PMS female subjects was employed for comparison purposes.

In their seminal, pioneering, and sensitive research into the non-PMS components of the menstrual cycle, the authors have successfully identified five other equally important phases of the cycle—Menstrual Syndrome (MS), Après Menstrual Syndrome (AMS), Pre-Ovulation Syndrome (POS), Ovulation Syndrome (OS), and Après Ovulation Syndrome (AOS). Subjects falling within these five non-PMS control groups in the latest round of PMS research have complained of the following symptoms: irritability, combativeness, hostility, depression, anxiety, hypersensitivity, tearfulness, physical discomfort, tension, increased appetite, intellectual impairment, and lethargy. The keen reader will note that the symptomatology revealed by the five non-PMS groups is surprisingly similar to that of the PMS group, a finding that underlines the importance of using control groups in experimental design.

As Figure 1 graphically depicts, our research found a cyclical menstruation pattern, progressing through six discrete stages correlating with disruptive behavioral and psychological symptoms. Based upon the principles of parsimony and heurism, the authors have chosen to identify this pattern as the "Female Undifferentiated Ugly Mood Syndrome (FUUMS)."

Future Directions

Being sensitive to the possibility that our work might be interpreted as sexist or anti-feminist, we wish to state categorically that this

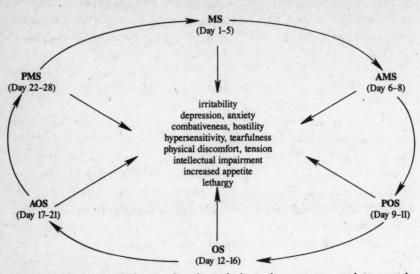

Figure 1. Disruptive behavioral and psychological patterns correlating with the six stages of the menstrual cycle.

accusation is not true. In fact, we are currently directing our research efforts at males in an attempt to better understand the male adjustment reaction to Female Undifferentiated Ugly Mood Syndrome. Our preliminary results show the following male reactive affective pattern: irritability, combativeness, hostility, depression, anxiety, hypersensitivity, tearfulness, physical discomfort, tension, increased appetite, intellectual impairment, and lethargy.

We believe we may be on the verge of discovering that what we had originally labeled as FUUMS may more accurately be termed UUUMS—Universal Undifferentiated Ugly Mood Syndrome. Should further research support this hypothesis, we feel we will have taken a great leap forward toward the goal of equality of the sexes.

References

Brauburn, D. D. (1973). *A good man is hard—no, make that impossible—to find.* Berkeley: Castrati Bros.

Crabbe, M. F. (1962). The martyr complex as a manifestation of the penoid personality disorder. *Journal of Fascinating Manhood, 4,* 369–370.

Kurse, G. D., Kramp, P. S., & Payne, A. (1960). *A friend indeed*. Belle Acres, WI: Midol Press.

Phleaux, E. Z. (1985). *Females in flux: A practical, self-help manual for going with the flow*. Waco, TX: Red River Publishing Co.

Porkas, B. F., & Hogge, B. F. (1975). *Hamming it up: A clinical handbook for the treatment of the porcine personality disorder*. Chicago: Oscar Meyer Publishing Co.

Ragg, O. T. (1958). *A bitch in time*. Piscataway, NJ: NcNasty Publishers.

Tex, K. O., Ponnz, T. M., & Doosh, C. F. (1981). The correlation between choice of menstrual paraphernalia and assertive behavior: A longitudinal study. *Journal of Radical Feminist Gynecology, 12,* 8–17.

628MIT: A Driving Tale
of Vehicular Maladjustment

Meredith G. Warshaw, M.S.S.
Frontier Science and Technology Research Foundation

Many examples of abuse and maltreatment are seen by mental health workers. The author presents here the psychosocial assessment of a particularly sad case in the hope that it will prove edifying to all who care for society's unfortunates.

Identifying Information

628MIT is an 8-year-old green Gremlin of AMC origin. It is an only car and was adopted 1 year ago after living in an unknown number of previous foster placements.

Presenting Problems

628MIT has been having severe somatic disturbances of late, necessitating extensive treatment, with a need for major surgery in the near future. Recently, it has become increasingly difficult to predict on a given day whether 628MIT will be willing to go out or not, and mobility and speed have become severely limited, resulting in an unwillingness to venture far from home.

Assessment of Current Psychosocial Functioning

628MIT is currently held in a joint custody arrangement between its adopted mother, Ms. W., and P. Garage. 628MIT resides with P.

Garage on alternate Mondays through Wednesdays, and Ms. W. pays (exorbitant) Gremlin support. 628MIT can be very communicative to those it trusts, but is unhappy around strangers.

Background History

628MIT's early life is unknown. Born in 1974, there is evidence of at least one accident requiring major cosmetic surgery. It is unknown how many homes it resided in previous to its current placement. Three days after adoption by Ms. W., 628MIT was hit by a cab, causing major disfigurement to its left side. Thereupon followed a long history of psychosomatic disorders, culminating in a nervous breakdown in the Callahan tunnel in Boston.

628MIT was very unhappy about moving from Boston to Philadelphia, feeling overburdened by the demands placed on it to haul heavy loads. It has never fully adjusted to its new home. This fall it developed major valve problems and can no longer move at full speed or power. Feeling overwhelmed by the winter, 628MIT seems to have lost all will to live.

Diagnostic Impression

DSM-III Axis I: Adjustment Reaction with Severe Psychosocial Stressors and Somatic Complaints.

Prognosis

628MIT is a very ill Gremlin, suffering from palpitations, hesitation, lack of energy, poor motor control, and broken valves. Major engine work will be needed to extend 628MIT's life more than a few months, but it is doubtful whether even that will bring it back to health and adequate functioning, or if it would just prolong 628MIT's agony. Sadly, 628MIT does not seem long for this world and it may be kindest to avoid heroic measures and allow it to die with dignity.

Adult Children of Normal Parents[1,2]

G. Sheldon Rusk, A.C.S.W.
Dayton Institute for Family Therapy

Today ample services are provided for those who suffer from the traditional forms of mental illness, chemical dependency, marital or family problems, and "nerves." But it has become increasingly apparent that we therapists ignore a large segment of society which is most in need of our help—those who have no one to blame but *themselves*—those who we professionals now identify as Adult Children of Normal Parents (ACNP—pronounced "a snap").

ACNPs are infrequently seen in the traditional therapies, are often forced to cope with life on their own terms (frequently relying on codependent children and/or spouse), and are stigmatized by security, financial success, happiness, and a pervasive sense of normalcy.

Review of the Literature

Cleaver (1958) has identified the onset of ACNP, which usually occurs during early adolescence when the attractiveness, popularity, good grades, and a supportive family are manifest in the young person's budding sense of self-confidence.

[1]This article was first presented as a paper to the American Society for the Study of Biomolecular Psychoproctology (ASSBMPP), Giardia Park, New Jersey, 1986.

[2]Adjunct faculty at the Dayton Institute for Family Therapy provided no help in the preparation of this article, whatever they may claim. My personal thanks to Andy Solovey for sharing his devastating experiences as an ACNP.

Grant and Hepburn (1938) noted that the seeds of competency are insidiously sown during infancy when basic trust is developed by parents who, seemingly without thinking, meet their child's emotional and physical needs with tender loving care. Walton (1979) remarked that these parents seem to have learned responsible, supportive parenting from their own parents, and speculated that there may be a multigenerational component to the development of an ACNP.

Course of Treatment

Occasionally seen in individual therapy, infrequently in family therapy, and never in group therapy (especially support groups), when they *are* seen, the ACNP clinically presents with some common life difficulty, such as an unexpected large inheritance. Other complaints noted by this author range from the serious (death of a significant parent) to the innocuous (fluctuation in the stock market). The course of therapy tends to be brief and when depth techniques such as confrontation are utilized, ACNPs invariably take responsibility for their own behavior, apply solutions which they claim work, and drop out of treatment with flimsy excuses like, "I'm fine, really!" This is a disappointing outcome for income, an obvious "flight into health."

One complaint seems to surface frequently and may be of interest to marital and sex therapists—the renewed romantic and concomitant sexual interest of the ACNP's spouse. Often this occurs when children successfully leave home and the couple has more time to themselves. But as Nelson and Nelson (1960) point out, this interest may not be as spontaneous as it appears. There is evidence that the spousal relationship had been warm and loving during the child-rearing years.

Borderline Normals

Many therapists complain that they do not get true ACNPs in treatment but see those persons now referred to as Borderline Normals (BNs—as opposed to BMs, or Borderline Mentals, that litter our caseloads). BNs present as being a little more bothered by their complaint(s), often stating that their first solution to their difficulty didn't work. Immediately they frustrate the therapist by asking for advice, then weighing the options before acting. Unlike BNs, true ACNPs provide solutions to their difficulties with frightening effectiveness and have no need to weigh options. Only with experience can the therapist make a differential diagnosis and decide whether or not to withhold advice until it is financially sufficient to give it.

Then there is the problem of transference and countertransference, especially when the ACNP sees the therapist as competent and supportive, or when the therapist believes him/herself to have had "normal parents." When either party starts to believe he/she is "normal," the therapy is in jeopardy.

Research Implications

Suspecting a biological/genetic component to ACNPs, the National Institute for Mental Illness has recently funded a twins research project which will study the Doublemint twins over a 10-year period to see if attractiveness can lead to financial security and correlate with happiness.

French researchers, looking into a viral causal agent for ACNPs (called a *paroquet*), are disputing American findings of normal brain scans in ACNP patients. One researcher pessimistically quips, "Of course the CAT scans appear normal—we don't know what we're looking for yet, do we?"

Preliminary findings by Dr. Jane Fondle's study of high-fiber diets of aerobically fit older ACNPs indicate that they live long and healthy lives. Doctors are now worried that a proliferation of ACNPs will result in a serious reduction of income-producing maladies.

Psychoeconomist Alex Keaton (1987) has coined what he calls the "Salad Bar Options" investment habits of ACNPs. They no longer rely on the traditional "passbook" savings account at 5.25% but prefer options with free, unlimited check-writing privileges.

Psychologist Jim Anderson, Jr. (1983) states that his father knew best how to measure the ACNP personality. He is currently testing a new instrument called Young's Universal Personal Prosperity Inventory and Experience Scale (YUPPIES). Anderson is so impressed with

YUPPIES that he will propose a new category for DSM-IV—Major Effective Disorders. Proposed diagnostic criteria are:

A. Competency, sense of security, financial success, and happiness.
B. *None* of the following: blaming parents for problems, blaming current therapist, conspicuous poverty, whining.

Medication

After initial failure by Dr. Gallo, Drs. Bartles and James, from the Napa Valley Clinic, have reported promising results in the use of medication in the treatment of ACNPs. C_2H_5OH, prescribed in liquid form, calms the pervasive mild anxieties that often accompany a successful life-style with few side effects.

This medication, either pale or dark red, if prescribed under a foreign name such as "cabernet sauvignon," is much favored by ACNPs. The age of the C_2H_5OH is much valued, and the older the medicine the greater the leverage when compliance with medication is an issue. Other ACNPs prefer yeast preparations of natural grains, insisting on drinking their medicine chilled between 40°F and 45°F.

Discussion

Existential therapists anguish over their inability to keep ACNPs in treatment, while hypnotherapists are entranced by the ACNPs' ability to generate large incomes. As mental health professionals, we must face that fact that, while Adult Children of Normal Parents comprise a large segment of society, *we will never be able to carry a larger mortgage because of them.* Sadly, I can still hear the sage advice of the late Dr. Milkem Erickson echo in my mind: "May my invoice go with you."

References

Anderson, Jim, Jr. (1983). YUPPIES. *Journal of Catalogue Shopping Psychometrics, 10*, 19-135.
Cleaver, Wally. (1958). Growing up normal. *Journal of Orthopsychosis, 1*, 13-18.

Grant, Cary, & Hepburn, Kate. (1938). Bringing up baby. *Journal of Zoolatry, 2,* 42–47.

Keaton, Alex. (1987). Money: The family tie that binds. *Family Largess, 87,* 234–239.

Nelson, Ozzie, & Nelson, Harriet. (1960). The Familial Cinéaste Syndrome. *Archives of General Psychobabble, 113,* 814–832.

Walton, John Boy. (1979). *The six fingers of Eve.* Deliverance, GA: Inbred Press.

4

Psychological Testing

On the Robustness of Psychological Test Instrumentation: Psychological Evaluation of the Dead

Jeri J. Goldman, Ph.D.

Dead subjects have heretofore been studied only retro-spectively, a grave error, particularly in view of the large size of the dead population. The present study rectifies this mortifying situation by applying the sophistication of modern-day testing and interviewing techniques, which permit interpretation even when no raw score or other response has arisen, to necronites. In addition to identifying those procedures best utilized for such subjects, findings indicate that necronites represent the dual-diagnosed condition—dead subjects are moderately to mildly retarded and emotionally disturbed. Implications for psychotherapeutic and educational intervention are discussed.

Psychological study of the dead is not a new field, but it has been reincarnated in recent years as the currently popular clinical exercise of the "psychological autopsy." Such studies necessarily come to a rather inconclusive dead end, however, since they all embody the rather benighted approach of resurrecting past history.

From the corpus of this extant literature, we have learned that dead persons have generally been more spirited and animated prior to their demise (Compose, 1965; Hume, 1979; Karloff, 1969); have an undying penchant for flowery obsequy, ritual, and ceremony (Bituary, 1980; Donne, 1623; Egy, 1956; Pottersfield, 1985; Reaper,

2001; Roget, 1852); display achievement anxiety over life's culmination (Heller, 1961; Prepared, 1984; Seuss, 1986; Skinner, 1983; Yorick, 1600); and definitely do not wear plaid (Martin, 1982).

Some light was also shed by the discovery that deceased individuals are gifted nyctalops (Horseman, 1820; Lugosi, 1982) and persuasive devil's advocates (Abolique & Diablo, 1692; Fernal, 1985). Reconstructionist studies have further revealed that the vocational interests of the deceased tend to cluster in the fields of medicine (Chaney, 1925; Frankenstein, 1984; Noguchi, 1983; Quincy, 1950), parapsychology (Katz, 1953; Murphy, 1965; Weiss & Houdini, 1926; Wolfeman, 1962), business (Iacocoon, 1984; Pluteau, 1929), and real estate (Cult, 1982; Dickens, 1861; Dostoyevsky, 1862; Gates, 1938; Mageddon, 1972). Avocational pursuits appear to emphasize travel (Alighieri, 1321; Lazarus, 33; Murphy, 1955; Peter, 67; Wilder, 1934), gourmandism (Antibodi, 1958; Bierce, 1914; Body, 1985), and various other aspects of "the good life" (Crepehanger, 1986; Fonda, 1986; Horseman, 1937; Lucifer, 1985; McCabre, 1962; Ruth, 1986).

This sparse, rather skeletal body of knowledge is, heaven knows, an appalling state of affairs, especially considering the size of the dead population, and a major, readily available source of data has inexplicably been overlooked by even die-hard researchers, leaving the field of study unnecessarily shrouded in darkness. This grave error has been the failure to undertake direct, personal psychological evaluations and mental status examinations of decedents, a procedure which is distinctly a live possibility with the sophisticated testing materials and probing interview techniques at the disposal of the modern-day researcher.

Special recognition should be given here to Wechsler, whose monumental Wechsler Adult Intelligence Scale—Revised (Wechsler, 1981) was heaven sent for this purpose, making it possible to assign IQ scores to subjects who make no score at all on the test. The WAIS-R thus joins an elite number of other, more narrowly focused psychological tests which also display this culture-free aspect, as will be seen later.

The present study rectifies the previous mortifying condition in the field of necrology by demonstrating the fact that dead men (and women) can indeed tell tales if proper testing instruments and skillful analysis of interview material are utilized, and by describing the psychological characteristics thus identified in deceased subjects.

Method

Subjects

Subjects were 666 necronites from all walks of life, applicants to a major cryogenic institute, examined on admission to the facility. Each voiced no objection to the study, no doubt volunteering for it as a means of killing time.

Procedure

Examiners were all seasoned clinicians, devil-may-care necromancers with much experience with other similarly lifeless groups, such as civil service employees, military draftees, and graduate students.

For the phase of the study concerned with formal psychological evaluation, comparisons were made to normative data of each test. For the phase involving mental status examinations, subjects were matched with a control group of college sophomores enrolled in an introductory psychology course, back-ward schizophrenics, and a tame strain of albino rats. Variables thus controlled included age, sex, pride, covetousness, lust, anger, gluttony, envy, and sloth.

Standard testing and interviewing procedures were utilized, with the exception that the subjects were permitted to recline, as they somewhat cryptically resisted being seated by the examiners' desks, feigning symptoms of syncope, narcolepsy, and somnolence, and hence slumping to the floor when efforts were made to have them remain seated. A carefully calibrated death watch was used to time the procedures, and scoring of tests was by skeleton key. Subjects were examined in the order in which their number was up.

Results and Discussion

Some testing procedures and materials proved to be of abysmally low power with dead subjects. These ineffective instruments included self-report inventories, paper-and-pencil tasks, and life-space interviews, however skillfully conducted. These procedures elicited no particular response from dead subjects, apparently because of failure to engage their interest and to arouse their motivation.

Observer rating scales of overt behavior yielded many more data, with encouraging reliability ($r = 1.00$, $p < .001$), and several psychometric devices proved quite applicable, as will be described below. Contraindicated in general were those testing instruments which require a raw score above zero and/or the establishment of some basal level of response—for example, the Stanford-Binet (Terman & Merrill, 1960)—as deceased subjects appeared dead-set against rising to these occasions and remained uninvolved with this type of assessment device, no doubt because of test-taking anxiety.

Intellectual functioning of dead subjects was found to range from moderately retarded to mildly retarded levels on the WAIS-R, by DSM-III (American Psychiatric Association, 1980) standards, varying somewhat as a function of age. Verbal IQ had a tendency to decrease somewhat during the late 20s to the early 30s, but dead subjects steadily recouped these losses with increasing maturity, until the regression disappeared by age 70, when original level of verbal intelligence was regained. Performance IQ in dead subjects showed a somewhat similar pattern, except that (a) regression in these skills reached its nadir slightly earlier in life (early 20s), and (b) losses were not only recouped, but indeed eventual performance skills by age 70 exceeded significantly (i.e., by 12 IQ points) their original level. These regressions in verbal and performance abilities were, of course, reflected in Full Scale IQ, which died away during the 20s and early 30s but also steadily rose to beyond its original level by age 70. Overall, it can readily be seen that dead subjects tend to get smarter with age, especially where their performance skills are concerned (see Table 1).

Academically, death has a somewhat similar effect, in that it obviously does not entirely interfere with functioning, although it did appear to cast a pall over skills, presenting something of an impediment. According to the Wide Range Achievement Test—Revised (Jastak & Wilkinson, 1984), dead subjects were below a third grade level in reading (recognition), spelling, and arithmetic, as they tended to achieve no raw scores. Other, more specific achievement tests suggested that dead subjects fare better in reading than they do in phonetic spelling or in arithmetic. (However, silent reading, especially of dead languages, is difficult to assess with confidence in deceased subjects.) On the Woodcock (Woodcock, 1973), for example, the dead subject was generally at a beginning first grade level in all measured independent reading skill areas, but was instructional at a

Table 1. WAIS-R Scores of Dead Subjects

Age	Verbal			Performance			Full Scale		
	RS	SS	IQ	RS	SS	IQ	RS	SS	IQ
16–17	0	6	54	0	5	49	0	11	46
18–19	0	6	52	0	5	48	0	11	45
20–24	0	6	50	0	5	47	0	11	<45
25–34	0	6	46	0	5	50	0	11	<45
35–44	0	6	49	0	5	54	0	11	47
45–54	0	6	51	0	5	57	0	11	48
55–64	0	6	52	0	5	59	0	11	49
65–69	0	6	53	0	5	60	0	11	50
70–74	0	6	54	0	5	61	0	11	51

Note. RS = raw score; SS = standard score.

slightly higher level and did not reach frustration level until somewhat more complex material was presented (see Table 2). In spelling, however, the dead subject's typical raw score of zero yielded a Spelling Age on the Test of Written Spelling (Larsen & Hammill, 1976) of less than 5-5 for predictable words (but of less than 7-5 for unpredictable ones), while a similar raw score on the KeyMath (Connolly, Nachtman, & Pritchett, 1976) produced a grade equivalent of less than .01. No hand preference was indicated on paper-and-pencil tasks, a dead giveaway that necronites are obviously ambidextrous.

In any event, it should be noted that the scholastic skills of necronites are generally at levels commensurate with their intellectual ability, a finding which has several important implications. To begin with, dead persons thus cannot be regarded as underachievers; apparently they do the best they can academically with the cognitive resources at their disposal. Instructional systems based on contracting and other forms of reward-punishment are therefore contraindicated as probably to little avail, and patently the necronite should not be made to feel at fault or blamed for lack of scholastic progress. Secondly, dead persons appear not to be "college material," although certainly university professors believe that there are a good many necronites enrolled in higher educational facilities today. Useful guides to potentially appropriate programs, however, have been provided by Siris (2700 B.C.), Nepenthe Institute (1961), and Dracula (6-5000). Finally, large amounts of public monies should probably not

Table 2. Woodcock Reading Mastery Tests (Forms A + B) of Dead Subjects

Subtest	Raw score	Easy reading level	Reading grade score	Failure reading level
Letter Identification	0	1.0	1.0	1.0
Word Identification	0	1.0	1.0	1.1
Word Attack	0	1.0	1.2	1.4
Word Comprehension	0	1.1	1.2	1.3
Passage Comprehension	0	1.0	1.1	1.2

be expended in such social programs as vocational rehabilitation and industrial retraining for necronites, as they are unlikely to benefit therefrom, although the rolls of such programs also appear to contain many such individuals already.

Overall adaptive functioning in dead subjects tended to be quite low. However, they were uniformly able to score points on the Vineland Social Maturity Scale (Doll, 1965) for such items as "Occupies self unattended" (Life Age = .35), "Does not drool" (Life Age = .90), and "Is left to care for self or others" (Life Age = 11.45). Depending on how vigorous a denial was required by the rater (necronites tended to display a stubborn dead silence), dead subjects were sometimes also credited with "Disavows literal Santa Claus" (Life Age =8.28), as they did not report such a belief, particularly if the subject was Jewish. Further, if the deceased was famous for good deeds, a point could be scored for "Advances general welfare" (Life Age = 25+ and at the top of the scale), inasmuch as it is past recognition which is the criterion for passage.

At the most, then, the dead subject tended to have a Social Age of 4 months (.30) on the VSMS, with Social Quotient of about 1 for those 25 years of age and over. However, as can be seen from the above item analysis, the adaptive functioning of the dead subject was erratic, with a considerable range of passage from a very low item to the very highest one, and a revealing pattern of "failing easy and passing difficult" items emerges, perhaps reflective of such conditions as learning disabilities, schizophrenia, multiple personality, or all of the above.

There were also rater problems in applying the VSMS to dead subjects, with many raters crediting the necronite with a perfect 300 score (and hence uppermost Social Age of 30+ and superior to very superior Social Quotients, inasmuch as "No Opportunity" scores were assigned to all items, "special restraint or lack of environmental opportunity or occasion" being seen as represented by a deceased condition). However, other, more conservative raters interpreted death as a "physical or mental disability," for which the VSMS disallows such "No Opportunity" scores. The solution to this lack of rater reliability on the VSMS appears to lie in more strenuous training for raters in the proper interpretation of Section 501 of the Rehabilitation Act.

Performance of dead subjects on projective measures tended toward a uniformity of substance and content which suggests an underlying, unidimensional character structure (Type Dead C Personality). There was a bland, dead-pan rejection of the projective stimuli, whether visual (Murray, 1943; Rorschach, 1921) or (dictated) auditory (Rotter, 1950) in nature, accompanied by low productivity, rigidity, and avoidance. Typically, dead subjects appeared buried in thought and did not even venture to touch any stimulus cards. On the Rorschach they tended not to display any creativity in rotating the cards to seek percepts, and their records were notably devoid of both such positive signs as movement responses and such pathognomonic indicators as color-naming. (However, there was a suggestion of unconscious pyrophobia.) Thematic Apperception Test (TAT) stories and Incomplete Sentence Blank (ISB) completions lacked personally meaningful, trenchant content (although TAT Card 16, the "blank card," holds promise); indeed, many outright rejections occurred. Such extreme blocking clearly categorized dead subjects as "repressers," rather than "sensitizers," and withdrawal into strong internal preoccupations is suggested.

Clinically, mental status examinations indicated that although oriented $\times$ 0, dead subjects were generally hypoactive, with serious psychomotor retardation and hypotonia accompanied by apparently elective mutism and the waxy flexibility of catatonia. Facies was usually dull and expressionless, and affect was flat and blunted. Latency of response was extreme. Severe problems existed with immediate, recent, and remote memory, to the point of amnesia, and retention of new learning appeared equally limited. Anorexia, neurasthenia, inhibited sexual desire, and a loss of interest in self-care, coupled with a dispirited, lifeless type of dysthymia, suggest a lack of healthy cathexis (Addams, 1962).

This apparently quite repressed state may make dead persons likely suicide risks, especially in view of their frequent recent preoccupation with death, typical lack of any future plans, and tendency to have written wills giving all their possessions away (Queath, 1986; Sufruct, 1985). The presence of apathy, "tracks," and pupil dilation also makes the astute clinician suspicious of considerable substance abuse, and many dead subjects are indeed believed to have significant underworld connections (Zebub, 1864). Obviously, there were many skeletons in the closets of such subjects, but they remained oblivious to examiner pyrotechnics designed to unearth these. To give the devil his due, it should be noted that necronites are consistently passive-aggressive, and even when observed together appeared to have little esprit de corps, simply assuming a live-and-let-live attitude.

Other clinical insights derived from these mental status procedures, albeit only with considerable spadework expended in listening with the third ear, suggest that necronites are probably inactively psychotic. Dead subjects were believed to be experiencing delusional states (with a paranoid flavor deduced from their fixed belief in plots), a persistent fantasy of having attended their own funerals, and an unhealthy preoccupation with the hereafter. In addition, dead subjects appeared to harbor many irrational fears, for which no earthly reason could be found: of particular birds and animals (such as vultures, hyenas, and jackals, which no doubt represent primitive totem figures) and of necrotomies (Quest, 1956), necrophagans, and necrophiliacs, as well as of archeologists, earthquakes, and urban renewal. Olfactory hallucination of the odor of sulfur dioxide also proved to be a grave marker of the condition.

Treatment implications of these findings are profound. Dead persons probably would tend not to be self-referrals, apparently regard symptoms as quite ego-syntonic, and are likely to be excessively, obstinately noncompliant (not unlike such other patients as sociopaths, paranoid personalities, and physicians) with treatment. As with these other groups, resistance to psychotherapy is probable, and prognosis is at best guarded.

However, in the event that the clinician is requested to treat a necronite, it is suggested that a thorough physical examination, including a complete neurologic work-up, first be secured, as it appears likely that subtle changes in the central nervous system may be influential, and deficiencies in other bodily systems may also be playing some role. Further, certain specific treatment approaches (such as biofeedback, encounter groups, and reflective counseling techniques) appear contraindicated, although others (such as implosive therapy and various relaxation and meditative strategies) seem promising.

Of all the treatment techniques in the clinician's armamentarium, traditional psychoanalysis seems best suited to the necronite, allowing for the use of the couch and proceeding at the patient's own slow pace. Nonetheless, the hardy analyst who embarks on such a course should probably not think in terms of "cure" and should be prepared for an analysis interminable, with all its inherent risks of fatigue, of frustration, and of critical peer review and rejection by third-party payers. It is recommended that sessions occur at cryogenic facilities in order to minimize negative countertransference (O'Dell, 1975). Of course, if cremation (Martyr, 35) has occurred, the patient will be more fragmented (Bearer, 1933; Wilde, 1895)—possibly even scattered (Sutt, 1980)—and therapeutic reintegration will be particularly difficult.

Conclusions

Dead subjects thus are clearly *not* untestable, as formerly believed. Despite their decedent status, and thanks to the miracles of modern sophistication in assessment techniques and instrumentation, necronites are able to score at moderately to mildly retarded levels on a standard intelligence test, at from about first to second grade on recognized achievement measures, and at erratic but wide-ranging levels of adaptive skills on a typical adaptive behavior scale; dead subjects behave consistently and should not be regarded as underachievers. However, they do appear to be seriously emotionally disturbed, with many signs of contributory organic impairment as well. Onset of the condition is believed to be acute, and it appears to represent a significant decrement from probable pre-morbid state, thus classifiable as a dementia. While prognosis is guarded, and no "cure" can reasonably be expected, traditional psychoanalysis interminable appears to be the treatment of choice.

Moreover, the age-old question of what exists after death has been laid to rest. Once necrosis occurs, what exists is neither heaven/hell nor a void. Instead, it has been demonstrated to be a state of mental retardation and emotional disturbance—and thus, in a nutshell, of dual diagnosis.

References

Abolique, D., & Diablo, L. (1692). The joy of hex. *Satanic Quarterly, 1,* 1–9.

Addams, C. (1962). One flew over the vulture's nest. *Village Vault, 2,* 10–19.

Alighieri, D. (1321). *Up the down stairway to heaven.* Hades: Purgatory Press.

American Psychiatric Association. (1980). *Diagnostic and statistical manual of mental disorders* (3rd ed.). Washington, DC: Author.

Antibodi, A. N. (1958). Suddenly, last summer. *Fiendish Digest, 3,* 20–29.

Bearer, P. (1933). Imitation of life: Remains to be seen. *Saturday Reviewing, 4,* 30–39.

Bierce, A. (1914). *Where there's a will, there's a wake: Gourmet cooking for the minyans.* Hell's Kitchen: Body & Soul.

Bituary, O. (1980). Ashes to ashes and dust to dust: It's your funeral—why not enjoy it? *Rolling Stoned, 5,* 40–49.

Body, M. (1985). *The man who mistook his wife for soul food and other culinary tales.* Donner Pass: Archives of Necrophagia.

Chaney, L. (1925). Phantom of the operating room. *Journal of Experimental Immortality, 6,* 50–59.

Compose, D. (1965). Until death do us party. In K. Addish & Y. Iskor (Eds.), *Manual of death-defying activities* (pp. 60–69). Molder: Elysium-Fields.

Connelly, A. J., Nachtman, W., & Pritchett, E. M. (1976). *KeyMath Diagnostic Arithmetic Test.* Circle Pines: American Guidance Service.

Crepehanger, A. (1986). Black is beautiful. *Charnel House Fashions, 7,* 70–79.

Cult, O. (1982). Paradise in earth: User's guide to lebensraum. *Real Estate Planning, 8,* 80–89.

Dickens, C. (1861). Great expectations. *Archives of Perpetual Care, 9,* 90–99.

Doll, E. A. (1965). *Vineland Social Maturity Scale.* Circle Pines: American Guidance Service.

Donne, J. (1623). Little knell of the olde sarcophagus shoppe. *Ossuary Annals, 10,* 100–109.

Dostoyevsky, F. M. (1862). *The house of the dead.* St. Elsewhere: Omega State University Press.

Dracula, C. (6-5000). *Everything you always wanted to know about sleep learning but were afraid to ask.* Transylvania: Somnialists' Almanac.

Egy, L., Logy, U., & Toll, X. (1956, January). *The last hurrah.* Paper presented at the annual convention of the Liars' Club, Nirvana.

Fernal, I. N. (1985). *Desperately seeking Satan.* Salem: McGraw-Hell.

Fonda, J. (1986). The anaerobic work-out: Dancing in the dark. *Journal of Nervous and Fatal Disease, 11*, 110–119.

Frankenstein, D. R. (1984). What they don't teach you at Harvard Medical School. *New England Journal of Mortality, 12*, 120–129.

Gates, P. (1938). All this and heaven, too. *Mother Earth News, 13*, 130–139.

Heller, J. (1961). *Catch 22: You can't take it with you*. Shangri-La: Orpheus Eurydice Jovanovich.

Horseman, H. (1820). Eyeless in Gaza. *Journal of Ghost Riding, 14*, 140–149.

Horsemen, 4. (1937). *A day at the races*. Apocalypse: Specter & Sons.

Hume, X. (1979). *Mummy dearest*. Cairo: Pyramid Press.

Iacocoon, L. (1984). How to succeed on the graveyard shift without really dying. *Necrology Today, 15*, 150–159.

Jastak, S., & Wilkinson, G. S. (1984). *The Wide Range Achievement Test—Revised*. Wilmington: Jastak Associates.

Karloff, B. (1969). *The relationship between activity level and decumbent status as a function of cessation of vital processes*. Unpublished doctoral dissertation. Requiem University, Coffin City.

Katz, M. (1953). *I led nine lives*. Karma: Poltergeist Publishing Co.

Larsen, S. C., & Hammill, D. D. (1976). *Test of Written Spelling*. Austin: Pro-Ed.

Lazarus, I. M. (33). *Palestine on $5 a day*. Jerusalem: Yortzeit University Press.

Lucifer, O. N. (1985). Gimme a light: The bier-barrel polka dirge. *Paris Match, 16*, 160–169.

Lugosi, B. (1982). First blood: Fly-by-night affairs for fun and profit. *Ladies Home Vampire, 17*, 170–179.

Mageddon, R. (1972). The grass is always greener over the bottomless pit. *Judgment Daily, 19*, 190–199.

Martin, S. (1982). Dead men don't wear plaid. *Harper's Bizarre, 20*, 200–209.

Martyr, A. (35). Arrivederci, Roma! *American Pyrologist, 21*, 210–219.

McCabre, A. M. (1962). Sex and the single ghoul. *International Journal of Tetrology, 18*, 180–189.

Murphy, A. (1955). *To hell and back*. Boothill: John Brown.

Murphy, B. (1965). *Is there death after life?* Brigadoon: Van Nostrum.

Murray, H. A. (1943). *Thematic Apperception Test*. Cambridge: Harvard University Press.

Nepenthe Institute for Continuing Education (1961). *Directory of college and other postmortem studies for cadavers*. Big Sur: Author.

Noguchi, T. (1983). *Morgue and Mindy*. Hollywood: D. A. Doornail & Sons.

O'Dell, D. (1975). Great moments in mortuary science. *Good Hearsekeeping, 22*, 220–229.

Peter, S. T. (67). *From here to eternity*. Rome: Charles Catacomb's Sons.

Pluteau, I. M. (1929). *How I made a million dollars in the Styx market*. Lake Woebegone: Charon, Cerberus, & Associates.

Pottersfield, I. N. (1985). I demand my rites! *Exceptional Embalmer, 23*, 230–239.

Prepared, B. (1984). Prudence, the Garlic Patch Doll. In Y. Knot (Ed.), *Just in casebook of chiropterophobia* (pp. 240–249). Kiddie City: Chant du Cigne Co.

Queath, B. (1986). *Will power!* Grave's End: Dee Press.

Quest, I. N. (1956). Invasion of the body snatchers. In *Gray's necrotomy* (pp. 250–259). Sepulcherville: Posthumous Press.

Quincy, T. V. (1950). *Kind hearts and coroners.* Los Angeles: University of Southern Crematoria Press.

Reaper, G. (2001). *A tisket, a tasket, a red and yellow casket.* Cemetery Ridge: Mortician Bros.

Roget, P. M. (1852). *Famous last words: Thirty days to a more powerful epitaph.* Tombstone: RIP.

Rorschach, H. (1921). *Psychodiagnostics.* Bern: Hans Huber.

Rotter, J. B. (1950). *Incomplete Sentences Blank.* New York: Harcourt Brace Jovanovich.

Ruth, D. R. (1986). Romancing the stone. *National Enquirer, 24*, 260–269.

Seuss, D. R. (1986). The grateful dead: You're only old once. *Newsletter of the United Mausoleum Fellowship, 25*, 270–279.

Siris, O. (2700 B.C.). Credit for life experience. *DOA Bulletin, 26*, 280–289.

Skinner, B. F. (1983). *La dolce vita: Enjoy old age.* Deadwood: Moribund State University Press.

Sufruct, U. (1985). Fame, fortune, and funerals. *Deadalas, 27*, 290–299.

Sutt, T. (1980). What causes acid rain? *Indian Journal of Crop Dusting, 28*, 300–309.

Terman, L. M., & Merrill, M. A. (1960). *Stanford-Binet Intelligence Scale* (3rd rev. ed., Form L-M). Boston: Houghton Mifflin Co.

Wechsler, D. (1981). *Wechsler Adult Intelligence Scale—Revised.* New York: Psychological Corporation.

Weiss, E., & Houdini, H. (1926). *They said it couldn't be done—and they were right!* Seance City: Bumrap Press.

Wild, O. (1895). *The importance of being urnest.* Asheville: Columbarium & Co.

Wilder, T. N. (1934). Heaven's my destination. *Journal of Consulting and Clinical Teleportation, 29*, 310–319.

Wolfeman, T. C. (1962). *Who's Afraid of Virginia Werewolf?* Silverado: Ghostbusters' Almanac.

Woodcock, R. W. (1973). *Woodcock Reading Mastery Tests.* Circle Pines: American Guidance Service.

Yorick, P. (1600). Nobody lives forever. *U.S. News and Worm Report, 30*, 320–329.

Zebub, B. L. (1864). Notes from the underground. In R. Kane (Ed.), *Handbook of comparative demonology* (pp. 330–339). Redux: Manifest Destiny Publications.

The Minnesota Multiphasic Personality Inventory (MMPI) Updated: 1988 Edition

Albert Rosen, Ph.D.

The Minnesota Multiphasic Personality Inventory (MMPI), with 566 true-or-false items, first appeared 45 years ago but is now sadly outdated. Based upon the weight of his vast clinical intuition, not to mention quite a bit of clinical experience as well, the author presents here revised items which he feels will greatly enhance the reliability and validity of this powerful personality measure.

Answer each item T(rue) or F(alse).

I am easily awakened by the firing of cannons.

I believe I am following others.

I was not very strict with my parents.

Most of the time I don't like to read newspaper articles about nuclear accidents nearby.

My sex life is satisfactory, except when I am with another person.

I am troubled by attacks of optimism.

I get nervous when I handle $100,000 bills.

It takes a lot of argument to convince most people that they are lying.

Sometimes I feel that things are real.

When I grow up I want to be a child.

I try to steal people's thoughts and ideas when they are not looking.

I believe that my home life is as miserable as that of most people I know.

I am afraid when I look down from the ground floor of a building.

I have many enemies who secretly love me.

There was too much love and companionship in my family

I am sexually attracted to beings from outer space.

As a youngster, I was usually suspended from school for attending.

I frequently notice that I am not trembling.

I have nightmares every day.

I am liked by most people, unless they know me.

I get happy easily and then can get over it soon.

I think I would like the work of a robot.

The Fabick Sexuality Survey—
Alternate Form (Form B)

Stephen D. Fabick, Ed.D.

Clinicians have oftentimes been faced with the difficult task of assessing the sexuality of their patients in objective ways which would not threaten to violate the American Psychological Association's Code of Ethical Principles of Psychologists. The need for a highly reliable and valid measure of human sexuality was finally met with the advent of the Fabick Sexuality Survey (Fabick, 1984). Many clinicians, however, have complained that, as with any repetitive task, the constant administration of the instrument results in a certain degree of boredom. Bearing the clinician's need for novelty in mind, the author presents here an alternate form of the Fabick Sexuality Survey.

1. Which of the following functions can lessen sexual spontaneity? (Circle all that apply.)
   a. illness
   b. drugs
   c. anxiety
   d. death
2. Fertilization of the egg usually occurs in the
   a. vagina
   b. Fallopian tubes
   c. uterus
   d. drive-in
3. Secrecy during copulation is characteristic of
   a. virtually all cultures
   b. only literate societies
   c. Presbyterians

4. Recognizable male and female genitalia appear in the
   a. first month of fetal development
   b. second month of fetal development
   c. third month of fetal development
   d. June issue of *Penthouse*
5. Full-blown homosexuality is
   a. on the increase in America
   b. twice as common in males as females
   c. a redundant term
6. A condom used alone is
   a. 99% effective
   b. as effective as a diaphragm and spermicide
   c. no fun
7. When a couple has difficulty with insufficient lubrication, they should consider using
   a. increased "foreplay"
   b. estrogen
   c. K-Y jelly
   d. Pennzoil 10W-40
8. Almost all women who report sleep-associated orgasm
   a. are oversexed
   b. have previously been orgasmic by other means
   c. get insufficient sexual satisfaction during waking hours
   d. should call my evening number

Reference

Fabick, S. D. (1984). Sexuality survey. *Journal of Polymorphous Perversity, 1*(2), 18–19.

Animal Movement on Rorschach Cards: An Empirical Analysis of a Deservedly Neglected Topic

Bruce A. Sorkin, Ph.D., and Thogeo F. Freylerp, Ph.D.
University of Maine

Psychologists have long used the Rorschach as a source of a few cheap laughs at the expense of their unsuspecting patients. Unknown to most psychologists, however, the Rorschach can also be used as a research instrument. The present experiment focuses on one of the long-standing controversies in the Rorschach literature—the meaning of animal movement responses on the Rorschach cards. Inspired by recent integrative work by others (Wachtel, 1977), the authors draw their methodology from a combination of psychoanalytic and learning perspectives.

The notion of integrating psychodynamic concepts with the experimental analysis of behavior is not new. It is known that Skinner asked Freud to co-author a second edition of *The Behavior of Organisms* (Skinner, 1938). Freud's portion of this manuscript was left incomplete, however, when he passive-aggressively died. In a tribute to Freud 2 years later, an undaunted Skinner (1940) gave us a hint of what might have been in his famous and popular (but now unavailable) paper, "Working Through the Transference Neurosis in Pigeons on a Concurrent Schedule: Implications for Change-over-Delay Parameters." The following year witnessed Skinner's struggle with metatheory in the form of another brilliant monograph (Skinner, 1941), *Regression in the Service of the Ego and Operant Conditioning: Isomorphic*

73

Constructs? Skinner refused, however, to submit it for publication, saying that his dog ate it.

Related developments in the 1950s included the preparation of a manuscript co-authored by Sidman and Menninger. Sadly, the pigeons under study developed brief reactive psychosis and unwittingly soiled the manuscript in their regression to anality.

Klopfer and Sender (1936) first discussed the importance of animal movement on the Rorschach. According to Exner (1974), this response uses both the determinants of movement and form and "... some of Rorschach's examples included animals in movement" (p. 75). There is, however, a great deal of disagreement among the members of the psychological community about the meaning of this response. There is also disagreement about the effect of colored cards on the response. Most experimenters agree that colored cards elicit more primitive responses reflecting primal instincts and are exemplified by animal movement responses (see, for example, the essay "Colored Cards Elicit More Primitive Responses Reflecting Primal Instincts and Are Exemplified by Animal Movement Responses," by U. B. Illin, 1946). The present research was designed to answer some of these questions by rigorous experimental means.

Method

Subjects

Subjects consisted of 100 male albino rats at a large undergraduate university recruited in the usual fashion. Rats were offered one experimental credit toward the four they needed to raise their course grade. They were also threatened with strychnine.

Procedure

Rats were randomly assigned to chromatic (Card IX) and achromatic (Card I) groups. They were placed on top of the Rorschach cards and their movement was measured in centimeters. During the time they were on the cards, they were exposed to an unpleasant stimulus, a 2-minute recording of the heavy metal group "Ratt" (we would like to thank the ethics committee member who, appalled, suggested we do this rather than drop heavy metal on the rats).

Results and Discussion

Rats on the colored cards moved at exactly the same rate as did rats on the achromatic cards, $t(99) = .53$, $p > .05$. Although at first blush this would not appear to support our experimental hypotheses, we believe that it actually does. The rats on the colored cards were obviously more excited and in-touch-with-their-essential-rat-being but they also used the ego defense of regression so that their behavior did not reflect this.

As a final note, according to Klopfer and Kelley (1942), animal movement on the Rorschach cards indicates that the subject "is emotionally infantile, living on a level of instinctive prompting below his chronologic and mental age" (p. 279). We could find no evidence to support this.

References

Exner, J. E. (1974). *The Rorschach: A comprehensive system.* New York: John Wiley & Sons.

Illin, U. B. (1946). Colored cards elicit more primitive responses reflecting primal instincts and are exemplified by animal movement responses. *Journal of Insulting and Cynical Psychology, 3,* 5–13.

Klopfer, B., & Kelley, D. M. (1942). *The Rorschach technique.* New York: World Book Co.

Klopfer, B., & Sender, S. (1936). A system of refined scoring symbols. *Rorschach Research Exchange, 1,* 19–22.

Sidman, M., & Menninger, K. (1955). Analysis of resistance in a stimulus-oddity-avoidance paradigm: The role of object loss in interresponse time per opportunity distributions. *International Journal of Behavioral Psychoanalysis, 10,* 103–111.

Skinner, B. F. (1938). *The behavior of organisms.* New York: Appleton-Century-Crofts.

Skinner, B. F. (1940). Working through the transference neurosis in pigeons on a concurrent schedule: Implications for change-over-delay parameters. *Journal of the Experimental Psychoanalysis of Behavior, 1,* 19–46.

Skinner, B. F. (1941). *Regression in the service of the ego and operant conditioning: Isomorphic constructs?* Unpublished manuscript. In Rover.

Wachtel, P. (1977). *Psychoanalysis and behavior therapy: Toward an integration.* New York: Basic Books.

The Friedberg Clinical Inventory: A Test of the Friedberg Personality Configuration

Robert D. Friedberg, Ph.D.
Center for Cognitive Therapy

Barbara A. Friedberg, M.S.
San Diego State University

Personality assessment is a growing area replete with opportunities in academia, clinical settings, and television game shows. However, while the field is expanding, the opportunities to become truly famous are rare (Terry, 1984). Terry noted that it helps to have something named after you if notoriety in psychology is desired. For this reason, the Friedberg Clinical Inventory was developed to assess the Friedberg Personality Configuration.[1] Although the Friedberg Personality Configuration is a relatively new (2 weeks and 15 minutes old) and rare (2 in 250–300 million) phenomenon, its identifying features can be culled from the Friedberg Clinical Inventory which is humbly presented below.

Circle the number that applies.

	Always	Sometimes			Never
I play fetch with myself.	5	4	3	2	1
Diarrhea runs in my family.	5	4	3	2	1

[1]Computer software is available for all PCs through Itza Byte, Inc. Interpretative programs provide floating and sinking profiles, recommendations for rehabilitation, and reviews of upcoming cable movies. Our programs are so user friendly that they invite you to dinner. Order now and receive the computer game, "The Friedbergs Meet Donkey Kong," FREE!

	Always	Sometimes			Never
I feel guilty after eating Jewish food.	5	4	3	2	1
I believe death is simply a change in life-style.	5	4	3	2	1
I wish my portrait were painted on velvet.	5	4	3	2	1
One or more of my family embarrass me.	5	4	3	2	1
I think bad karma can be countered by a powerful anti-perspirant.	5	4	3	2	1
I enjoy giving myself hernia check-ups.	5	4	3	2	1
Complaining is my favorite aerobic exercise	5	4	3	2	1
Holiday visits with my in-laws are my favorite contact sports.	5	4	3	2	1
I am suspicious of the 7 Dwarfs' relationship with Snow White.	5	4	3	2	1
I fantasize about being marooned on a desert island with an Elvis impersonator.	5	4	3	2	1
I eat out of a satellite dish.	5	4	3	2	1
I have the urge to hunt Audubon Society members.	5	4	3	2	1
I'd like to see my dentist's picture on the back of a milk carton.	5	4	3	2	1
I enjoy smelling other people's shoes.	5	4	3	2	1
I worry that when the Martians invade earth there won't be enough parking spaces.	5	4	3	2	1
I astral travel during sex.	5	4	3	2	1
Geraldo Rivera searches for me.	5	4	3	2	1
I have trouble discriminating between "always," "sometimes," and "never."	5	4	3	2	1

Reference

Terry, W. S. (1984). Prescriptions for fame in the history of psychology. *Journal of Polymorphous Perversity, 1*(2), 15–17.

5
Clinical Psychology

Clinical Psychology and the Scientist-Practitioner Model: The Ultimate Solution

E. U. Reka, Ph.D.
Boulder University

Clinical psychology's ideal model, that of the scientist-practitioner, has long resisted exact expression and implementation. With the landmark formulations presented here, however, this ineffable model readily yields its secrets.

Much has been said and written affirming clinical psychology's continuing espousal of the scientist-practitioner model. Translating its philosophy into an action plan, however, has remained up until now an elusive goal, difficult to quantify and to assess. The author, working under a year's fellowship at the Edsel Foundation Center for Advanced Study in the Behavioral Sciences, has been able to discover ten immutable scientific laws relevant to the scientist-practitioner model and to devise their expression in mathematical formulae. The results of this major breakthrough are presented below.

First Law of the Conservation of Psychic Energy

Where ego was, there shall id be; usually observed in a client immediately following a psychotherapy session in which you feel that you finally *are* getting somewhere and have bragged to a colleague about it.

$$E = Id^2$$

Second Law of the Conservation of Psychic Energy

As there are only a finite number of IQ points in the universe, an increase in the score of one client, usually someone else's, is accompanied by an opposite and exactly equal decrease in the score(s) of one or more other clients, usually yours.

$$IQ = K$$
$$\therefore IQ_1 + N = IQ_2 - N$$

First Law of Thermodynamics

The number of referral reports received is to their legibility as your loss of visual acuity is to your frustration tolerance.

$$\uparrow N_{rr} : \downarrow L_{rr} :: \uparrow L_{va} : \downarrow T_f$$

Second Law of Thermodynamics

A client's Obnoxiousness Quotient is approximately equal to the sum of his/her repetition compulsion and resistance to suggestion, when multiplied by negative bill-paying behavior.

$$OQ_c \approx (RC_c + RS_c)\,(-BPB_c)$$

First Law of Gravity

The pressure of the waiting list for testing is much greater than the combined heights, weights, IQs, salaries, Social Security numbers, and basal metabolism rates of the staff psychologists in a given organizational setting.

$$P_{wl_t} \geqslant N_\Psi \frac{(H + W + IQ + \$ + SSN + BMR)}{N}$$

Second Law of Gravity

The Vocational Interest Score of a given case conference is inversely proportional to your need to use the bathroom.

$$\text{VIS}_{cc} \propto \text{N}_{ach_{pp}}$$

First Law of Measurement

The universe of interpretations of a given Rorschach response is identical to the number of angels which can dance on the head of a Kuder Preference Record pin.

$$U_{R_r} \equiv \frac{DA}{P_{KPR}}$$

Second Law of Measurement

The Social Quotient of a given client in a residential treatment center always exceeds his/her IQ when houseparent experience with him/her is less than the houseparent's 90-day probationary period.

$$E_{hp} \not> 90 \text{ days}$$
$$\therefore SQ_c \gg IQ_c$$

First Law of the Fourth Dimension

The perceived length of time of a psychotherapy session varies directly with the amount of negative countertransference experienced by the therapist.

$$X_p \propto -CT_t$$

Second Law of the Fourth Dimension

The length of time required to complete a report of a client's annual review (IEP/IHP) is a direct and covariant function of the number of participants in the team conference and the amount of teacher resistance to producing a written evaluation, when combined with the team secretary's Procrastination Quotient.

$$X_{r_{ar}} \propto N_p + R_t + PQ_s$$

Like all Great Truths which, once enunciated, become immediately obvious, these principles will doubtless be readily confirmed by astute clinicians everywhere. Doubtless also, the inherent heuristic value of these laws will generate many corollary principles, a spate of hypothesis-testing, and, at last, hard data. Psychology has thus finally become a true and unified science, equally exact in the office as in the maze. More importantly, a major schism in the American Psychological Association (APA) can now be averted and those prejudicial special assessments that have been levied by the APA on practitioners thus rescinded.

Jeri J. Goldman, Ph.D.
The Woods Schools & Residential Treatment Center
Langhorne, Pennsylvania

6

Neuropsychology and Neurology

More Clinical Tales: The Man Who Mistook His Wife for a Dishwasher

Richard Liebmann-Smith

When she came into my clinic, Mrs. R. appeared to be a pleasant, slightly plump 35-year-old woman. Her blood lipids, urine protein, cerebrospinal fluid, EEG, CAT scan, and PET scan were all normal.

"Doctor, it's about my *husband*," she finally said.

Mrs. R. then proceeded to describe a situation so incredible, so far beyond the routine bizarreness to which all neurologists become inured, that I had no clinical choice but to invite myself to dinner that very evening.

Surprisingly, like his wife, Mr. R. (Chuck) proved to be a perfectly pleasant, slightly plump 35-year-old. Throughout a lavish and lovingly prepared repast, he revealed himself to be a most charming and cultivated dinner companion, regaling me with an amusing and perceptive disquisition on the early Mnemonist painters and displaying a thorough—even encyclopedic—familiarity with the prime numbers. Schopenhauer himself, I couldn't help but think, would have been delighted with his company. There was not the slightest hint in this lovely chap's demeanor, in short, to provide any adumbration of the harrowing postprandial behavioral abyss into which he was about to plunge willy-nilly.

Indeed, it was only after we were well into the dessert course—a mouth-watering *tarte tatin* that Sartre would have thoroughly enjoyed—that the ominous possibility of "something wrong" began to register on my diagnostic antennae. At that juncture there lay on the table the full detritus of a fabulous five-course dinner: sticky silverware, plates glazed with *sauce choron*, wineglasses rubied with the residual sediment of choice vintage Bordeaux, and more.

Surely, I thought, Mr. R. will now rise, excuse himself, clear the table, and head toward the kitchen to do the dishes. Instead, to my mounting dread and disbelief, he motioned expansively toward the den and invited me to join him there for cigars, cognac, and perhaps a little routine neurological testing.

I must have looked aghast. What kind of mad, barmy, topsy-turvy, lunatic, Alice in Wonderland dream world was he living in?

"But who will do the dishes?" I blurted without thinking—a question that would have been unbelievably cruel had Chuck R. the slightest awareness of his blatant impairment.

"Hey, no problem," he rejoined with chilling nonchalance. "Babs'll take care of them."

Nothing in my vast clinical, psychophysical, phenomenological, or philosophical experience could have prepared me for the extraordinary condition of Chuck R. While his mind seemed to have effortlessly grasped the notion of a dish as *something to eat off* (he had, after all, managed to deal with everything from the fruit-cocktail cup to the cake plate without the slightest trace of confusion), the concept of a dish as *something to wash and dry later on* was apparently absolutely alien to his being. His wife had shopped, cooked, set the table, and was even now beginning to clear it. Did he really expect the poor woman to do the dishes as well? (Even Nietzsche, I imagined, would have offered at least to do the wineglasses.) Yet it was clear that the thought that he should perform any such compensatory labor, however inadequate, simply never entered Chuck R.'s skull.

Through the distorting lens of the amber nectar in my upraised brandy snifter, I gazed around the den. Within my visual field was a VCR, a personal computer, and a cordless telephone. But despite all these reassuring accoutrements of contemporary culture, I realized that Mr. R. was helplessly frozen in some past epoch, trapped like a pathetic prehistoric mammoth in the glacial deposits of a grotesque TV-sitcom version of a world that had moved on without him.

Postscript

Since originally publishing the strange case of Mr. R., I have been made aware of a surprising number of similar syndromes in the neurological literature. I am especially indebted to Dr. Emma Porter for calling my attention to the almost comically enantiomorphic behavior of a patient in her own practice, a woman who mistook her husband for a lawnmower.

A Prodigy Lost

Throughout human history, the appearance of child prodigies has been perceived as a portent of the supernatural, heralding a rent in the familiar fabric of existence. As such, these precocious composers, rapid calculators, and chess masters have always inspired an edgy admixture of awe and fear in those who encounter them. Yet it was with something more like mild irritation that I greeted the appearance of little Timmy M. in our clinic. The tiny tyke, sitting across from me with an air of petulant abstraction, seemed anything but prodigious. He paid almost no attention to my questions, answering, if at all, with barely audible grunts. In response to even such simple neurological tests as my sticking his legs with pins, he became surly and uncooperative. In short, he appeared to be nothing more than a perfectly normal 6-year-old child.

I was on the verge of dismissing him from my office when I became uncomfortably aware that little Timmy's attention was riveted on my neck. The sullen mask of his subpubescent face was entirely transformed into a keen, almost predatory expression of demonic intensity. Wittgenstein, I thought, would have been scared out of his wits.

"Isn't that an epidermoid cyst?" piped Timmy, pointing to a small bump just below the line of my luxuriant beard.

I was astounded that the child could have noticed this minuscule blemish from the distance that separated us, much less that he could have diagnosed it accurately. Just a few days previously, I had consulted a world-renowned dermatologist about that very condition. And what the distinguished medical personage had told me on that occasion was virtually *word for word* what now emerged from this strange child's mouth.

"It's nothing to be concerned about," said little Timmy. "These things are benign. You can live with them for the rest of your life without trouble so long as they don't become infected. But if you'd like to have it removed for cosmetic reasons I can do it under a local and have you out of here in less than an hour."

I decided to keep the little fellow in the clinic for further observation.

For the rest of the day I tried to put this disturbing conversation out of my mind, but it all came flooding back that evening when, by chance, I was passing the children's ward on the way to dinner. It was the glint of some highly polished metallic object that caught my attention. Wishing not to be observed, I stole behind the slide and began to watch what soon proved to be an utterly magical and spontaneous scene. There was little Timmy, a look of fierce concentration on his face, performing an emergency appendectomy on one of the other little children. Dumbfounded, I watched the 6-year-old wonder deftly excise the inflamed vestigial organ with flawless technique. Other tots in the ward had somehow been instructed by this juvenile Aesculapius and, properly scrubbed and dressed in infant-size gowns, gloves, and masks, were performing all the functions of a well-trained O.R. team.

Nothing I had learned in neurology, neuropsychology, or cognitive biosociology could begin to account for this extraordinary surgical "knack" in a child who had yet to master the intricacies of a two-wheeler. In virtually every other instance of which I was aware, such finely honed surgical acumen was the result of a minimum of 4 years of medical school, followed by at least as long a stint in an accredited surgical-residency program. Yet Timmy M.—by virtue of his age and undistinguished performance in kindergarten—could scarcely have arrived at his phenomenal abilities by any such conventional route.

What then could have given rise to this remarkable "symptom"? In a single year, beginning on his fifth birthday (as I soon ascertained), Timmy had performed dozens of successful surgical procedures in his playroom O.R., ranging from simple tucks and face-lifts for his mother's friends to a total hip replacement for his uncle and a triple coronary bypass for his grandmother. If Timmy was sick, we did not even have a name for such a healing illness.

Postscript

The practicing neurologist never fails to wonder at the remarkable plasticity of the human cerebral cortex. No sooner had I adjusted to the reality of Timmy M.'s unprecedented surgical skills than they evaporated as mysteriously as they had arisen—to be supplanted, however, by something far more bizarre, far less savory.

Only a week after entering our clinic, Timmy became sulky and secretive. He no longer took pleasure in hide-and-seek or in neurosurgical rounds, and he refused to perform even the most uncomplicated tonsillectomy. Rather, he was observed to spend nearly all of his time in his room, where I found him one evening engaged in a strange and solitary ritual. On the bed before him was spread out a pile of papers, which I naturally took to be patients' charts. Yet when I inquired what brilliant new diagnoses he was coming up with, Timmy shook his head and sheepishly handed me the top sheet. The handwriting on it was the childish scrawl of a 6-year-old, but what I read on the page was clearly the product of a fully formed literary sensibility:

> Wordlessly she implored my surgical succor—her dark Keanean eyes pools of unplumbed anguish as she gestured to her lower-right abdominal quadrant. Haunting stanzas from the immortal Bemelmans' seminal "Madeline" flickered through my consciousness. "And soon after Dr. Cohn/came, he rushed out to the phone/ and he dialed: DANton-ten-six—/'Nurse,' he said, 'it's an appendix!'" And indeed it *was* an appendix—the most violently inflamed specimen of that troublesome appendage I had heretofore encountered. As Malraux has told us . . .

Timmy's prognosis, I now saw, was bleak. Whatever strange convolution of the infrafollicular cleft of his temporal lobe had originally driven him to wield a scalpel with such precocious precision was now compelling him *to write about it!* It was Chekhov's disease—the dread doctor-poet syndrome, now no longer rare but still one of the most intractable conditions in all of medicine. Timmy, I realized sadly, was beyond the ministrations of the neurologist, the psychoneuroimmunologist, or the developmental neuropsychiatrist. His only hope was to find an agent.

Toward a Psychology of Anaesthesia: Numbness Therapy

Howard M. Grindlinger, M.D.

While it is true that those who fail to examine history are doomed to repeat it, ignorance is bliss. Patients generally seek treatment in order to gain symptomatic relief from psychic pain. Therapists, on the other hand, seek to strip the patient of his/her defenses in an effort to enhance the patient's self-awareness, with little regard for the pain and suffering that comes with such increased awareness. Frequently, therapists must drug their patients because of the pain iatrogenically induced. This awareness process, then, seems both contradictory and cruel. An alternate and more humane approach to the treatment of patients seems called for. The author outlines in the present paper a new and more humanistic approach to the therapeutic treatment of patients—Numbness Therapy—with simple goals— anaesthesia and oblivion. As outlined below, the techniques of Numbness Therapy involve simple exercises, inexpensive and effective devices, short and pleasant sessions with a likeable therapist, and no drugs.

Stage I—Arterial Blocking Exercises

After explaining the rationale of seeking anaesthesia and oblivion, a series of exercises is described to and practiced by the patient/client, who can become adept within only 5 to 10 minutes. These are *Arterial Blocking Exercises.*

By positioning the limbs in such a manner as to block the flow of blood into these limbs, all circulation will be cut off and anaesthesia will be induced. The classical lotus position is perfect for obliterating all feeling in the lower limbs. Hanging the arms over the back of a chair while sitting in the chair produces a delightful anaesthesia of the upper extremities within 10 minutes.

Facial and cerebral anaesthesia is more complex and involves the partial occlusion of the common carotid arteries. While the procedure will be discussed below, only those advanced students enrolled in reputable Numbness Therapy centers should attempt its practice.

In review, the common carotid arteries arise from the aorta and carry oxygenated blood. They then branch into the external carotids, which supply the face and scalp, while the internal carotids supply the brain. The brain is split into two hemispheres, left and right, with each hemisphere controlling the opposite side of the body. The *right* internal carotid, then, supplies brain areas controlling *left* sided sensation and motor activity. The *left* internal carotid is responsible for *right* body side functioning, as well as its great import as supplier to the *speech* center. This presents some difficulties, to be discussed later.

The common carotid arteries lie to either side of the larynx (voice box). Thus, they are easily accessible to pressure created by the fingers of a trained hand. Compression of the *right* carotid results in a carefree spinning feeling and loss of sensation and motor activity for the entire *left* side. In addition, sensation to the *right* side of the face is also abolished. One can readily see the therapeutic advantage of *right* carotid compression, done while sitting in the lotus position, on a chair with free arm hung over the chair's back.

The major complication of carotid blocking is cerebrovascular accidents, or stroke. Unfortunately, strokes originating from occlusion of the *left* carotid would almost certainly involve the speech center. As mutism is a more frustrating situation than *left* cerebral and *right* body awareness, *left* carotid blocking exercises have been eliminated from the therapeutic armamentarium. We do not believe that utilization of the one *right* carotid in any way jeopardizes our therapeutic efficacy. However, as the *right* carotid suplies the *left* hand, the ten percent (10%) of the population that is left-handed might become crippled for life and must be duly informed. Other minor complications, such as cardiac arrhythmias (abnormal heart rhythms) and blood pressure problems, are handled through careful screening.

Stage II—Insentient Apparel

The second phase of therapy involves the purchase and use of *insentient apparel*. These are bullet-proof suits, similar to those worn by police officers, but are special in that they have been impregnated with a topical anaesthetic and instantly render the skin numb. Thus, all sensations are eliminated. Because these suits are made of dozens of layers of impenetrable, yet completely impregnated, nylon, they last a lifetime. Furthermore, *insentient apparel*, especially worn on the face and *right* side of the body, in addition to *right* carotid occlusion, substitute adequately for the deficiencies resulting from the inter-diction against *left* carotid occlusion. *Insentient apparel* is exactly tai-lored, quite stylish, and would in no way interfere with any corpo-rate dress codes. If one controls one's weight, such apparel could bring years of anaesthesia, right until the final oblivion.

Stage III—Experimental
Cortico-Corporal Separation

After mastering the *arterial blocking exercises* and incorporating regular periods of wearing *insentient apparel* into one's daily routine, patients/ clients are ready for the final phase of treatment. Taking our cue from television, we have developed a device that, when properly implanted into the correct area of the brain—the thalamus—will effect complete separation of mind and body, or *cortico-corporal separation*.

As we know, the thalamus is the switch yard of the brain, directing neural impulses traveling from the peripheral body to var-ious higher brain centers and directing neural messages originating in the brain to the appropriate parts of the body. Our implant counters all incoming stimuli to the brain, while blocking all impulses attempting to exit the brain on their way to the body. What is achieved is total, temporary (because the implant has a timing de-vice), neurologic oblivion.

Contrary to the thoughts of amateurs reviving Eastern philo-sophical practices, it is *more*, rather than less, mind-body separation that makes for improved, relaxed living. Such separation allows the body to go about the business of metabolism which it has been effectively programmed to do through millions of evolutionary years. The implant allows the body to do this without the interference of a poorly informed, ambivalent, fickle, and neurotic brain. Relief from bodily responsibilities relaxes the overworked and overstimulated mind.

The precise location of the implant is assured through microneurosurgical technique and guarantees the preservation of breathing, digestion, cardiac, and endocrine gland control. The operation is simple and involves the mere insertion of a tiny needle into the thalamic part of the brain, a procedure not too dissimilar from ones carried out by high school students on frogs. Of course, all patients are anaesthetized. A control unit is given to the patient, who can then select intervals ranging from 20 seconds to 2 minutes of mindbody separation. The timer responds instantly and shuts off automatically, bringing the individual back from the environs of oblivion. Our early research efforts have shown that those patients who have been involved with daily commuting on public transportation have been especially grateful for their implants.

While we have complete faith in our technique, the current sample (*cohort*) population is small and the duration of their implant use is short. Our data are, thus, too inconclusive to label this technique as anything but experimental.

Conclusions and Summary

Numbness Therapy is based on the concept that awareness is pain and that anaesthesia and oblivion are the most compassionate states a therapist may offer to a suffering patient/client.

The three stages of technique that are used have qualities of simplicity and conservation of time and expense. They are (1) *Arterial Blocking Exercises*, (2) *Insentient Apparel*, and (3) *Cortico-Corporal Separation*.

The therapy is completely organic and safe, in the right hands. Once the methods are learned, control is entirely in the hands of the individual, eliminating unwarranted interference from or liability to the therapist. No drugs are used. The patient acquires none of the iatrogenic side effects of prescribed medication, and none of the severe medical complications and social stigmata of illicit drug abuse. There is no burden to society. The patient is as functional as he/she wishes to be, all completely independent of momentary voyages into the soothing seas of anaesthesia and oblivion.

Know Your Neuropsychologist: An Eclectic Psychoeducational Intervention to Decrease Patients' Resistance to Neuropsychological Testing

Laura G. Kogan, Psy.D., and B. Sol Ganglia, Ph.D.
Jacques Lalobe Cortical Fitness Centre

Corrie D. Plexus
Neurorama Rehabilitation World, Inc.

It is a distressing but oft-observed truth that neuropsychologists become distracted by their patients' resistance to the testing procedures. Whining behavior, frequent expressions of fatigue and/or exasperation, as well as demands for excessive bathroom breaks, are clearly disruptive to the positive working alliance required for valid test administration. It is obvious that some patients have tremendous difficulty accepting the length, and, in private settings, the well-deserved fee which justly attends the professionally executed neuropsychological assessment.

Psychoeducational interventions have been found effective in dealing with resistance to various forms of therapy (Heinz, 1983; Money, 1985), although such strategies have not yet been attempted in dealing with the resistance engendered by lengthy and/or expensive psychological assessment procedures. Based on the hypothesis that patients would manifest greater tolerance for lengthy testing sessions if they were properly prepared for these procedures, we have devised specialized, empirically based psychoeducational materials for our patients. Preliminary analysis of 35 patients in a private center for neuropsychological assessment indicates that this intervention does facilitate compliance with testing procedures as well as prompt payment of bills.

Materials

Research has suggested that psychoeducational approaches are more effective when they are flexibly designed to accommodate individuals' particular learning styles and preferences (Washington, 1987). With handicapped patients referred for neuropsychological assessment, the proper choice of an educational medium becomes particularly critical. Our psychoeducational materials are commercially available in a variety of formats, to optimize a patient's ability to learn, and to retain information critical to the successful completion of testing. At present, our program "Know Your Neuropsychologist" is available in regular pamphlet format, in large-print pamphlet format for visually impaired patients, in a single right-column pamphlet form for deaf patients with left-sided neglect, in regular 15-minute audio cassette format for patients with cortical blindness, in rapid 3-minute cassette format for patients with hyperactivity or Attention Deficit Disorder, and in slow, 25-minute cassette format for patients with dementia. We are presently preparing a video format for patients from the TV generation. Prior to their first interview and testing session, all our patients are familiarized with our "Know Your Neuropsychologist" program. The version that follows includes footnotes, elucidating for our fellow professionals the psychoeducational strategies, empirically derived from the behavioral, dynamic, and family systems literature, which have rendered our program so uniquely effective.

Know Your Neuropsychologist:
A Pamphlet for Patients

What Can Your Neuropsychologist Do for You?

Much as your local car inspector checks your brakes, lights, and horn to make sure your car is in safe working order, so your neuropsychologist will learn about your brain by employing a variety of specialized techniques.[1] Some readers may be capable of wondering how a neuropsychologist can become so intimately acquainted with a brain during the course of a neuropsychological assessment. This is an excellent question: in fact, your neuropsychologist is simply testing the range and the limits of your abilities in many areas, much as your high school gym teacher challenged your strength, stamina, and courage by asking you to leap farther and farther during the long jump, until you finally landed head first in the sand pit. Your neuropsychologist is professionally trained to gather the information you need to help you win a major lawsuit, a disability case, or to help you get the veterans benefits you deserve.[2] In the event that you are interested in working, you can also ask your neuropsychologist for vocational or academic guidance.[3]

Do *not* expect your neuropsychologist to explain exactly what happens in your brain to elicit certain thoughts or feelings, such as intrusive sexual fantasies about your hairdresser, or wanton impulses to unleash your dog amidst your neighbor's geraniums. No reputable scientist will claim to understand exactly how the mind works, although research in this area is becoming increasingly sophisticated.

Getting to Know Each Other: The First Interview

Do not be alarmed if some of your neuropsychologist's initial questions seem peculiar: this is his/her own peculiar way of showing that s/he finds you interesting and unique.[4] It is important

---

[1] This technique of using an appropriate, educational metaphor is drawn from Occip et al.'s (1973) work on Analogico-Metaphorico-Semantic reasoning in 6-month-old chimpanzees, later adopted by Xanthia Seracks (1981, personal communication) in her psychoeducational work with patients suffering from anxiety disorders.

[2] Positive reinforcement for compliance.

[3] Creating an open, permissive working alliance.

[4] Cognitive reframing to reduce cognitive dissonance.

to answer all questions as truthfully as possible. If your neuropsychologist thinks you may be deviating from the truth, s/he may decide to supplement your neuropsychological testing with personality testing, which could add another 2-3 hours to your test battery.[5] Worse yet, if you pretend to have forgotten the answers, your neuropsychologist might give you the wrong diagnosis which, in extreme cases, can result in your having to consult a lawyer, an ill-fated situation at best.[5]

Challenging Your Brain: Neuropsychological Testing

During the examination, your neuropsychologist is like a dedicated ethnologist who has just discovered a new species of mammal: s/he will want to spend hours learning everything about the way you think, move, see, hear, feel, and communicate. So, your neuropsychologist will delight in observing how well you can stick out your tongue, sing, or write nonsense words from dictation. You will also have the opportunity to play with blocks and jigsaw puzzles, pour make-believe drinks into make-believe cups, and to engage in other activities which you enjoyed in kindergarten. Remember that your neuropsychologist is employing these powerful techniques to learn about your brain.[6]

If you want your neuropsychologist to do his/her best in your behalf, then use certain strategies that some of our patients have found to be particularly helpful. Some try to pretend that they are the psychologist during the testing session trying to learn as much as they can about their neuropsychologist.[7] If you try this strategy, you will observe that your neuropsychologist is very meticulous about details, seems to repeat each task numerous times, and takes many notes. Try on this obsessive style, as if you were trying on a new suit. Or pretend you are the devoted student of a Zen master, and focus your entire humble being on successfully accomplishing your neuropsychologist's every directive.[8]

Concluding the Testing

At some unspecifiable time in the future, your neuropsychological evaluation will come to an end. Remember that although you

[5]Negative reinforcement for lack of compliance.

[6]Impressing the patient with doctor's superior knowledge and status.

[7]Drawn from behavioral role-playing techniques, stress inoculation training, and psychodrama.

[8]Pure manipulation.

have worked hard for many hours, or possibly days, your neuropsychologist will expect you to pay for your evaluation. It's best to accept this inevitable reality.[9]

Getting Feedback From Your Neuropsychologist

Once s/he has interpreted your test results, your neuropsychologist will gladly give you feedback on your test performance. S/he may well tell you that the results were inconclusive and that s/he would like you to return for repeat testing in a few months. Patients who care about their health always express pleasure at this opportunity to return for further assessment.[10]

IF YOU HAVE ANY QUESTIONS, CONSULT YOUR NEAREST NEUROPSYCHOLOGIST

[9]Reality Therapy.

[10]Paradoxical intervention, leaving patient the choice of either complying, or neglecting his/her health.

References

Heinz, C. (1983). Use of the "plugged-up ketchup bottle" metaphor in eliminating bulimic patients' resistance to therapy. *Journal of Undesirable Behaviors, 12,* 66–91.

Money, D. (1985). Preparing fourth grade students for the client role: A community intervention study. *International Journal of Perfectly Normal Child Development, 15,* 12–46.

Occip, E., Et, A., & Al, L. (1973). Analogico-metaphorico-semantic reasoning in 6-month-old chimpanzees. In A. L. Front (Ed.), *Bringing up baby: How to increase your child's IQ in 18 years of intensive training* (pp. 9–10). New York: Dunce Press Inc.

Washington, D. C. (1987). Experimental utilization of illustrated, large-print informative materials for politicians. *Annals of Psycho-socio-politico Research, 18,* 1–17.

7

Educational Psychology and Education

On the Academic Speech: Quick and Easy Guidelines to the Disguise of Ignorance

J. Haskell, Ph.D.
University of London

As academics are called upon to speak before peers and students, it is important that they sound well-informed and thoughtful. This would be easy if they were well-informed and thoughtful, but requires too much time and effort. So, the question is how to appear up-to-date, innovative, and intelligent when you're not. Can you impress your students and, more importantly, your colleagues without knowing what the hell you're talking about? Of course you can! It's just a matter of knowing what to say and, equally important, what not to say. Once you are able to give a thoughtful, intelligent 90-minute lecture on a topic about which you know nothing, you're in line for promotion. If you can disguise your utter ignorance of a topic at hand for 3 hours or more, you're on your way to becoming a Full Professor. If you can stretch it to 10 or 12 hours, you can write a book! And if your ignorance is boundless and interdisciplinary, you can become a top administrator at a major university. Others have done it, so can you!

What follows are some quick and easy guidelines to the disguise of ignorance, as well as a Universal Academic Speech which you can use when needed. You can also create your own speech using the handy guidelines for reference. But remember: Practice will improve your ability to keep from your audience your complete lack of understanding of the topic.

Guidelines for the Disguise of Ignorance

1. Always note that the issue (problem, question) is more complex than it appears to be to others. Emphasize the long historical origins of the problem and its economic and social underpinnings.

2. Point out that all the greatest thinkers from Aristotle onward have contemplated the problem and have never arrived at a satisfactory answer. Modestly propose one.

3. Never give a straightforward response to a question. After all, if the problem is always more complex than it appears on the surface, a rapid reply indicates you haven't considered all the implications of the question. A request for the correct time, for example, might lead to a discussion of the concept of time, the notion of backwards time in physics, the futility of causal concepts in science and philosophy, a lecture on horology. Whatever strikes your fancy. It will help if, prior to responding to a question, you take a minute to stare at the ceiling, as if in deep contemplation.

4. Note the surprising number of distinguished colleagues who still maintain that the problem is unidimensional and can be removed from its broader context. Emphasize that this approach is unprofitable and has gotten us nowhere. By taking a multidimensional or interdisciplinary perspective, you place yourself in the front ranks of those concerned with the issue. (But see Corollary 1 below.)

> Corollary 1. If the current approach to the problem already is a multidimensional or interdisciplinary one, stress how divisive this is and propose a simple unidimensional interpretation. Liken this to Newton's unification of science.

5. Always let your audience know that you went to the University of Michigan or another Big Ten university (unless you really have a first-class education). Saying you were at Princeton might raise an eyebrow or two, with others possibly expecting you to know a friend of a friend of theirs who was in "your" class. The good thing about Big Ten universities is that they really are big. You couldn't possibly know everyone in your advanced graduate seminar, let alone your graduating class. So if someone's cousin was there at the time you claim to have been, you couldn't be expected to know them.

6. If your topic is one where you might reasonably be expected to be familiar with the research literature, note that the research has been poorly designed and is, from your point of view, virtually useless. Then mention a personal anecdote or two, noting that these

are more realistic and three-dimensional than all the research on the subject put together.

7. Note that you have not been allotted enough time to discuss all the implications of your assessment of the problem. This is the appropriate place to mention your latest book, order forms for which are available immediately following your talk. Of course, your book contains a much more detailed analysis of the subject. This device not only sells books but forestalls any embarrassing questions you may be called upon to answer.

Now that you know some of the basics of giving a thoughtful-sounding academic speech, let's see how these principles might work in practice. Below is a sample universal speech for a social scientist speaking to an audience of colleagues.

Sample Universal Academic Speech:
Social Science Version

Anyone who has thought about the issue [problem, question] for more than a moment will recognize that it is much more complex than most people assume and than I, myself, first believed when I was attracted to the subject as a graduate student at the University of Michigan. Sadly, even today, many of my colleagues consider the problem to be a unidimensional one, a position that I believe is a roadblock to progress. It is clear to me that the problem cuts across traditional boundaries, and as I have been saying for some time now, we must open our eyes to the fact that it is a multidimensional, multilayered, interdisciplinary issue. If we fail to examine it in its larger context we will never come to grips with it.

I know it is unfashionable these days to talk of interdisciplinary and multidi-mensional models, to speak of the sociohistorical and economic context in which this problem must be seen. People have always been attracted to simple, and dare I say simple-minded, explanations. But there are occasionally scholars, and I count myself among them, who are bold enough to point out the emperor's stark nakedness. Remember what they did to Socrates. To Galileo. To Kurt Waldheim. Unlike my colleagues, I am not content to examine this issue in the unnatural isolation of the university laboratory. We should not drag the problem, kicking and screaming, through the narrow doors of our laboratories. Instead, we must go out in search of the subject where it resides, in its native habitat. Only in this way can we perceive it in all its natural complexity. [Important: Wait for applause to subside before continuing.]

There has been surprisingly little research on this topic, despite its interest to philosophers and scientists throughout history. And much of what research there is is woefully inadequate in conception, design, and execution. Because the research is so inadequate, and hence, so little is really known about the problem, I will discuss an example from my personal experience. This is one of those rare instances where anecdotes are more informative than empirical research.

Not long ago I was on the train, on my way to give a talk at a major university. As I was looking over my notes, the delightful woman sitting next to me began a conversation. "Are you a scientist?" she asked, glancing at the notes on my lap. "Yes," I laughed, "a social scientist." "Sounds like a contradiction in terms," she added. I told her about the problem I was studying and about the research my colleagues had done to understand it. "It sounds like a waste of time," she replied, "and a waste of taxpayers' money." And she is right. The way that my colleagues squander research grants and graduate student talent in their parochial approach to the subject is incomprehensible. That is why I have never been tempted to apply for a research grant to study this issue. An unorthodox approach would never get funded because of the "old guard" who run the show.

Given how little we know about the problem, how can it ever be solved? First, we must recognize that the problem is multidimensional and, therefore, requires an elaborate explanation. Of course we do not know nearly enough at this stage to tackle the problem head-on. Those proposals that have been made deal with the problem on only the most superficial level. These proposals do not attack the root causes of the problem, the long historical development of the problem over many decades, and the social and economic context in which it must be viewed. I know that sociobiologists have recently proposed that the problem has biological origins and, therefore, cannot be eliminated no matter what we do. But today's sociobiologists are tomorrow's alchemists, turning everything they touch into DNA. The Band-Aid approach, which we have been using for far too long, can only prolong the problem, letting it fester until it becomes a terminal illness, unresponsive to any but the most radical surgery.

Time does not permit me to present any of the finer details of what I envision as the solution to this long-standing problem. Clues to my position may be found in my book, The Problem and Its Solution: Speculation and (Big-Ten) Educated Guesswork. I have a few postage-paid order forms here if anyone is interested.

I want to thank you for inviting me to give this brief overview of my most recent thinking about what I'm sure we all agree by now is an interesting and complex issue.

A Subjective Assessment of the Oral Doctoral Defense Process in Psychology: I Don't Feel Like Going Into It, If You Want to Know the Truth

Holden Caulfield, Ph.D.

If you really want to hear about it, the first thing you'll probably want to know is what my independent variables were, and what I was measuring, and what sort of covariates and all I used during the analyses, and all that Campbell and Stanley kind of crap, but I don't feel like going into it, if you want to know the truth. In the first place, the design wasn't all that interesting, and in the second place, once you've spent 2 years on something like that you sorta want to get it all behind you and think about something else. I'll just tell you about this madman stuff that happened to me last year about the time I was defending my dissertation and getting my lousy Ph.D.

Where I want to start telling is the day I had scheduled my oral defense. We're supposed to show that after spending about a hundred years researching and collecting data and analyzing and writing it up and all, that we can remember enough about it to spend 2 hours talking about it in some little room that smells like someone just took a leak in the corner. Personally I wasn't too crazy about the idea on account of it seemed like a waste of everyone's time. Especially mine, when what I really needed to do was to pad my vita and try to find some sort of goddam job. I was supposed to fly out for a job talk the next day and all and sort of had that on the old brain. But this oral defense business was some sort of Graduate College rule naturally, just like it's some sort of rule that the goddam margins on the document have to be exactly one and three quarters inches or something crazy like that. Oral defense. Strictly for the birds.

Anyway, so we're all in this lousy little room, everyone sitting around the table looking solemn as hell. My main advisor was there smirking a lot and making a hell of an effort to say a lot of witty things to break the mood, but it wasn't working. There were four other people I knew from my department, and then there was one guy I'd never seen before, this guy who the Graduate College assigned to my committee for the defense. He introduced himself as Professor so-and-so from the Economics department, and told us he wasn't feeling all that well and maybe had the grippe. That didn't make me feel too gorgeous myself, especially since he'd just spent about 5 minutes shaking my hand. He smelled like Vicks Nose Drops and had this very damp-looking handkerchief sticking out of the pocket of this very sad, ratty old jacket that he was probably born in or something. I wasn't too crazy about being in the same room with him if you want to know the truth.

Then to make it worse he started telling me all about Economics and how a good psychologist can really make a contribution if they have the right background. He kept telling me about this psychologist he knew and the pot of dough he'd made in Economics. The thing is, all the research I'd been doing wasn't anything like what he was talking about. He was some little cheerer upper. Goddam money. It always ends up making you blue as hell.

So I started talking about my dissertation. I had sort of prepared what I wanted to say, but it turned out I was having a lot of trouble concentrating. For one thing, I was hungry as hell. I had thought about maybe bringing a box of doughnuts into the defense with me, and passing it around, but I wasn't in the mood. You gotta be in the right mood for those things. And besides, I wasn't too crazy about the idea of explaining a big-ass factorial design with my mouth full of chocolate crullers or something. Another reason I couldn't really concentrate was the reason I already told you, that after 2 years of work I sorta wanted to forget about this project and move on. I'm always thinking of about a million ideas for other experiments when I should be finishing up the ones I'm working on. It's a lousy habit, I admit it, but I always do that.

But I think the biggest reason I couldn't really concentrate on the defense was that I was thinking about that goddam job interview. I was pretty worried about the job market, all of a sudden. I had about a million applications out, but I kept thinking that maybe I shoulda gone into English grad school after all. But I know I would have regretted that. I would have had to put up with a lot of very tall round-shouldered guys talking in these very bored voices about Proust or Joyce or somebody to prove what intellectual bastards they are. What phonies. People were always giving me advice. People were always telling me to look into industry. One guy kept telling me that the big money was in marketing. But I just couldn't see me in a marketing position. All these phony lean-jawed guys named David cleaning their fingernails and chewing the fat with a lot of phony girls named Linda or Marcia or something. Boy, you couldn't pay me to take a marketing job. I'm not kidding. Another thing I didn't want was to have to teach about a dozen courses at some tiny little college in the middle of nowhere and get no research done. Not that I expected to be snapped up by goddam Berkeley or anything, for Chrissakes. I wasn't all that excited about the job possibilities if you want to know the truth. About the only good advice I think I received was from someone who told me that if I knew my statistics there'd always be jobs for me. If you're a good statistician, she said, people will be calling you up night and day. Night and day—that killed me.

Anyway, I finally finished presenting my dissertation and then my committee started firing questions at me. Especially the guy from Economics. The way he'd do it was, he'd start with about 50 corny jokes, just to show me what a regular guy he was. Then he'd sort of blow his nose for a while and then state the question really slowly, punctuated with a lot of sniffs and coughs. It was pretty sickening in a way. It took him about 20 minutes just to ask a question. And when he'd finally finish phrasing his question he'd give me this icy look, like he'd just beaten hell out of me in Ping-Pong or something. I kept thinking about the job market and it was making me feel all sad and lonesome. Also I had this idea for an experiment on the old brain and what I really wanted to do was get the hell out of there and work on it.

So finally there were no more questions and they asked me to step outside. I wanted to check something in this one article for that idea I had, so like a madman I ran down the stairs to my office. Some stupid bastard had thrown peanut shells all over the goddam steps and I damn near broke my crazy neck. And just about the time I got back to the conference room my advisor and everyone else came out and started congratulating me and shaking my hand and calling me

"Doctor Caulfield" and all. Very big deal. The Economics guy was blowing his nose all over the place and slapping me on the back like I'd just won the goddam Olympics or something. It was kind of nauseating, if you want to know the truth. He told me not to worry about getting a job, that something would turn up. "After all," he said, "you've got a Ph.D." Witty bastard. All I meet are witty bastards.

We were all going to go off and get a drink, but the Economics guy started looking at his watch a lot and decided he couldn't make it. He apologized like a madman, but I wasn't too goddam sorry to see him go. He took off down the hall. He was halfway out the door when he turned around and yelled "Good Luck!" at me. I hope not. I hope to hell not. I'd never yell "Good Luck!" at anybody, especially a recent psychology Ph.D. It sounds terrible, when you think about it.

Mark Schaller, M.A.
Arizona State University

With apologies to J. D. Salinger. The author would like to thank Edge Egerton for his inspiration and insight.

The Chron-cm: A Quantitative Measure of Status in Academia

John B. Pittenger, Ph.D.
University of Arkansas at Little Rock

The Chron-cm, an index of the size of job advertisements printed in *The Chronicle of Higher Education,* is proposed as a measure of status of college and university employees. Data collected from an issue of *The Chronicle* were used to validate the measure and to test the Intensity of Student Contact Hypothesis of status loss.

It is extremely difficult to develop valid, qualitative measures of social status. This problem is especially severe in academia, where so many people compete for so little status. A recent letter to *The Chronicle of Higher Education* (Woodring, 1988) hints at a potential measure. Woodring pointed out that advertisements for college presidents were quite large, those for deans were smaller, and those for faculty (except for appointments to foreign universities such as Papua New Guinea) were smaller still. This, he suggested, gives the impression that the only people of real importance in American universities are the administrators. Having formed the same impression myself, albeit on other grounds, it seemed worthwhile to develop a quantitative measure of ad size and test its validity as a measure of status.

The Chron-cm is defined as 1 centimeter of vertical length in a one-column-wide ad in *The Chronicle.* For ads at the bottom of *The Chronicle*'s employment section (the ones in the microscopic type—hereinafter referred to as "microtype") the Chron-cm value is simply the length of the ad, since these ads are invariably one column wide. For the boxed ads (with large type, decorative borders, university seals, etc.) the length in centimeters was multiplied by the ad's width in number of columns. Thus, a box 2.5 cm long and 3 columns wide would measure as 7.5 Chron-cms.

For the May 4, 1988, issue of *The Chronicle* the Chron-cm scores of the ads were measured and recorded, with data separated along three variables: (1) U.S. versus foreign universities, (2) microtype versus boxed ads, and (3) job category. Job categorization was difficult and the following simple scheme was used for this initial test of the new metric. "Faculty" included all teaching jobs, regardless of rank and tenurability. "Deans" included ads for deans, assistant deans, and associate deans, even if the deanship was for a nonacademic position (e.g., dean of students). "Directors" included any job with director in the title (including associate directors, etc.). Registrars were also included in this category. "Librarians" included all librarians and archivists, except directors of libraries. "Chairs" included department chairmen, chairpersons, and department heads. "Athletics" included coaches, teacher-coaches, trainers, etc., but not directors of athletics or faculty appointments without coaching duties. "Presidents" included presidents, chancellors, vice presidents, etc. Given the metastasis of mid- to lower-level administrative positions in the last decade, it seemed best to lump the rest of the administrative ads into one category: "Assorted Administrators." "Psychologists" included both faculty appointments and a few counseling positions. Note that this category overlaps with "Faculty." Finally, in cases where an ad included multiple positions, the Chron-cm score for the whole ad was divided by the number of positions.

The resulting distributions are largely as one might have predicted, though with a few surprises. Data of U.S. institutions will be discussed first. It is reasonable to suppose that microtype ads, regardless of Chron-cm scores, indicate lower status than boxed ads. Observe in Table 1 that Faculty, Psychologists, Athletics, Librarians, and Assorted Administrators all have a majority of microtype ads while the others have a majority of boxed ads.

Table 2 presents the mean Chron-cm measurements by job category and ad type. For microtype ads notice that all means are small, indicating low status for this type of ad, except for the 10.0 found in the "President" category. This anomalous mean was based on a single ad for a president. Since no university would knowingly inflict such degradation on its president, the ad may have been put in microtype by accident. Alternatively, it may have been placed by one

Table 1. Frequency of Job Categories by Ad Type

| | | | | | Job category | | | | |
| | | | | | Department | | | Assorted | |
Ad type	Faculty	Psychologists	Athletics	Librarians	Chairs	Deans	Presidents	Administ.	Directors
Microtype	233	8	23	59	8	5	1	48	36
Boxed	152	8	4	11	14	32	27	29	79

Table 2. Mean Chron-cms of Job Advertisements by Job Category and Ad Type

Ad type	Job category							
	Faculty	Psychologists	Athletics	Librarians	Department Chairs	Deans	Presidents	Assorted Administ.	Directors
Microtype	3.9	4.4	5.3	6.3	5.7	5.5	10.0	4.5	4.4
Boxed	7.5	7.8	17.8	16.7	16.7	18.4	22.2	17.8	16.8

of the school's vice presidents who hoped to get the job by default, believing that no one else would apply for such a debased presidency.

Faculty have the lowest mean of all categories. This finding is, of course, crucial: If any category scored lower than Faculty, the validity of the Chron-cm as a measure of status would have been wholly invalidated. Some comfort to readers of this journal may be found in the fact that Psychologists average a bit better than Faculty.

The means for the boxed ads form three clusters. Presidents are off by themselves at the high end, Faculty and Psychologists isolated far down at the lower end (though, again, with Psychologists slightly higher), while the rest of the categories are grouped closely together in the middle. Notice the mean Chron-cms in boxed ads for all categories, except Faculty and Psychologists, are more than double the Chron-cms for the corresponding microtype and means. Why does status for Faculty and Psychologists not show a big increase in the presumably high-status boxed ads? The answer is simple: In most boxed ads for faculty, multiple positions are announced in a single box, thus avoiding the cost of duplicating the school's mailing address, affirmative action statement, etc.

The fairest way to measure status, however, is to compute means over all ads. These means are presented in Figure 1. These data can be used to test the Intensity of Student Contact Hypothesis: Among academics, status is inversely related to the intensity of contact with students. To those familiar with life on campus, it is obvious that student contact is most intense among faculty, less among chairs, even less among deans, and nearly nonexistent among presidents. Librarians who aren't directors also might be expected to fit the hypothesis—they are actually involved in educating students and (for some reason unfathomable to me) have fought to be granted

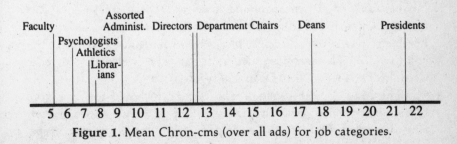

Figure 1. Mean Chron-cms (over all ads) for job categories.

faculty rank. They would appear to have less intense contact with students than faculty (no sections of 100 Intro students) but frequently deal with students on a one-to-one basis. The fact that their observed mean Chron-cm scores are higher than Faculty but lower than Chairs is, therefore, consistent with the hypothesis.

The low Chron-cm scores for Athletics may appear to invalidate the measure. Coaches are often paid more than presidents, are allowed to make embarrassing public statements, throw furniture, etc., all of which indicate high status. However, note that positions for *real coaches* (i.e., of football and men's basketball teams) are too important to advertise publicly. The athletics positions appearing in *The Chronicle* are usually for coaches of women's teams and such marginal sports as volleyball and tennis. (While NCAA requires such activities to be provided, it is not mandatory to take them seriously.) Many of these positions even involve teaching responsibilities. Thus, their status is low, consistent with their Chron-cm scores.

I was stunned to see that Directors were not only below Deans but even a bit below Chairs. This seemed anomalous. Directors *are* administrators and generally have (unlike Deans and Chairmen) rarely been contaminated by intense contact with students. How could their status scores be so low? A more careful inspection of the ads suggests that recent trends in title inflation are responsible. Many low- to middle-level administrative positions now carry the title of Director (e.g., residence director, associate director of admissions for continuing education, etc.). This may be a ploy by presidents to award status in lieu of an adequate salary.

If the Chron-cm metric is a ratio scale, some additional insight into the workings of status in academia can be observed. While it has long been known that flight from the classroom raises an academic's status, it has previously been impossible to state exactly how much of an increase is afforded by any particular promotion. Computing ratios among Chron-cm means shows that a move from strictly faculty rank to chairpersonhood gives a 110% increase in status (ratio of Chair mean to Faculty mean is 2.1), while leaps to Dean or President give 190% and 360% increases. Among administrative positions status increases are much more modest: Chair to Dean, 40%, Chair to President, 70%, Dean to President, 20%.

The May 4, 1988, issue of *The Chronicle* included few ads from foreign institutions. However, though limited, the data are as Woodring suggested. Only a couple of ads for faculty were in microtype, while 27 were in boxes. In spite of the fact that one university stuffed 10 positions into a single box, the mean Chron-cm scores of boxed ads for faculty was 11.1, well above the U.S. average.

Overall, the Chron-cm index appears to have been validated. Phrased more informally, the results turned out to match my preconceptions. Given this validation, my preconceptions can now be viewed as predictions and the results interpreted as empirical confirmation of my predictions.

More research needs to be done. Replications using other issues of *The Chronicle* would be valuable. I, myself, shall perform no replications. To do so would run the risk of finding results incompatible with my preconceptions. In any case, it might be worth considering more subtle variants of the measure: taking into account the size and variety of fonts in boxed ads, floridness of the description of amenities of campus life, whether or not the university seal or a picturesque campus building is displayed, etc. In addition, *Monitor-cms* could be measured in the APA *Monitor* to compare the status among categories of psychologists—academic versus private practice versus industry and, within universities, experimental versus applied, etc. If the APA actually gets around to reorganizing itself, such data might prove a useful empirical basis for deciding how to allocate power.

A final note. My colleague, Dr. Roger Webb, has suggested that the Chron-cm is actually an inverse measure of the level of desperation among job seekers. That is, university presidents wouldn't deign to read microtype ads, while members of the professoriate, especially recent Ph.D.s and chronic visiting professors, are desperate enough to burrow through any number of small-print ads. I expect Webb is right, but would argue that low status and desperation are causally related. Thus, the Chron-cm can validly measure both status and desperation.

Reference

Woodring, P. (1988, May 4). Are only administrators of real importance? *The Chronicle of Higher Education*, p. B5.

The Influence of Being Untenured on the Willingness to Submit Meaningless Replies: A Reply to Polloway

James R. Cook, Ph.D., Jo Ann Lee, Ph.D.,
Faye E. Sultan, Ph.D., and Arnie Cann, Ph.D.[1]
University of North Carolina at Charlotte

Polloway (1986), in a recent attack on the tenure system in universities, implies that tenure may result in the sudden decrease in productivity of faculty. [*Editor's Note*: The body of Polloway's article was completely blank.] He seems to suggest a negative relationship, with possible detrimental effects for the profession. We find this proposal, if that is what he meant, and we are not sure, poorly justified and counter to the best interests of the profession. We believe, and hope others agree, that the literature in psychology is growing at an alarming rate. It is no longer possible for an individual to thoughtfully consider all new findings. If granting tenure does in fact decrease productivity, we see this as a positive result. Granting tenure may be the only fair way to keep some professionals from clogging the journals with meaningless, or at least trivial, research reports.

There are other equally insightful comments we could make concerning Polloway's article, but we have two other manuscripts to get into the mail this afternoon.

---

[1]Cann actually did all the work, but he is tenured so he was listed last. Sultan does not know she is a co-author, but is untenured, so we thought she would want to be listed. Address reprint requests to Anyone But Sultan, Psychology, UNCC, USA.

Reference

Polloway, E. A. (1986). The influence of tenure on the productivity of faculty in higher education. *Journal of Polymorphous Perversity*, 3 (2), 7.

Student-Faculty Interaction Relating to Letters of Recommendation for Admission to Doctoral Programs: A Case Study

Larry Lister, D.S.W.
University of Hawaii School of Social Work

Thomas Jones, M.S.W.
Veterans Home of California

Letters of recommendation form a crucial component of the supporting materials upon which doctoral programs base their admission decisions. In asking a faculty member for a letter of recommendation, the student does not come from a position of power. Therefore, it is most important that he/she approach the faculty member in a diplomatic fashion, presenting his/her positive side while sincerely and sensitively portraying his/her need for a good recommendation, based upon past demonstrated accomplishments in class. Unfortunately, there is little in the literature to guide the student in just how to go about approaching this delicate matter of formally requesting a letter of recommendation from a faculty member. The authors present here a paradigm which the junior author utilized successfully in approaching the senior author for a letter of recommendation (see Figure 1). For didactic purposes, the senior author's letter of recommendation is also included to vividly illustrate how a carefully prepared request for a letter of recommendation elicited an equally thoughtful response (see Figure 2).

Dear dDr. Lister,

Hi! I hope you remember me. I was in too of your classses and was also at that great studnet-faculty party'y you had. I was the one who told you all of those funny ethnic jokes and realy got the party going. After those minority people left, I told some realy funny jokes that I got out of Screw magazine. You probably remember the guy who passed out the stuff that was suppose to be cocaine but turned out to be baking soda. Some people said it had PCP in it, but I thought it was just baking soda. Anyhow, it was still a great party wasn't it? And I guess you remember the guy who barfed all over your new sofa. Well, that guy was me.

Anyhow, Larry, (we no each other well enough to forgo the formrality of "doctor" and all of that) anyhow, I was wondering if you'd write me a realy great letter of reccomendation. I no I got incompletes in both of your classes, but that was because I got the clap a few times, and I had to study hard in those other cldasses so as not to get to many D's. You wouldn't have wanted me to put all of my time and efort into just your class, would you, Larry? No, of coarse you wouldn't. I new how you'd feel and tried to be sensitive to it.

You will be glad to no, Larry, that I've been practising that empathy stuff that one of the profs tried to teach us. YI'm working full time now at a famous car sales business. I even where a suit and tie now, YLarry! I look people in the eyes, smile, use there first names and try to make them feel good about themselves and there new cars. You might say, Larry, that YI was the social work representitive at the car lot. I bring care-alot to the car-lot. (Ha-ha, that was a joke, Larry. You remember what a good sense of humor I had)?

Well, Larry, I'm going to go to this neat school in California called the University of Infinite Studys. I'll be in the Doctor of Inrtegrative Processes (D.I.P.) program. I'm going to learn how yoga is the same as prsychology and social work and then they/'ll give me a doctorate. I was thinking that I could use yoga for car sales, to. Like Cal Worthington says, "I will stand upon my head to beat all deals". (another joke, Larry. Ha-ha).

So I hope you will write me a realy neat letter, Larry, or just sign the one YI/'ve enclosed and send it back to me. If you write a new one, put it into an unsealed envelop and then into a large folder and mail it to me. After I read it, I'll sned it to the sxchool and even pay the posrtage. that way I'll help you proof read it, Larry And the school will get it and think it came straight from you. they don't like if for us to proof read our letters of referance, but I think we should help each other out. You no, I'll scrratch your back if you'll scratch mine. Besides, I didn't sign away my rright to look at my letters of referance. I think people should perserve all of their rights. That's part of our profesional éthics, right/

Anyhow, Lary, I'll be glad to help you out, so write to me right away okay? Hey, you're sure a great guy, Larry!

Your's wityh care and compasion,

Thomas Jones, MS.W.

Figure 1. A sample letter from a student requesting a letter of recommendation from a faculty member.

California International University
of
Advanced Conceptual Theory and Family Therapy

Corner of Hibiscus Lane & Surf Street
Laguna Beach, CA 92666
Serving the academic community of Southern California since 1977

Yes, we take Visa
and MasterCard!

We offer 3% discount
on all cash payments.

To Whom It May Concern:

A Mr. Tom Jones has contacted me for a reference in connection with his application to your University of Infinite Studies. As I recall, Mr. Jones was a student in two of my classes several years ago. Mine were highly technical and theoretical courses dealing with the general principles of life. I am not quite sure how Mr. Jones was able to enroll without taking the prerequisites, but I do recall that an ingratiating manner and the promise of the loan of a Mercedes seemed to have an unusual influence over me at the time.

My records indicate that Mr. Jones wrote a paper for my course in which he attempted to relate ideas of interpersonal helping to their relevance in the market place. Mr. Jones was at that time moonlighting at the car lot of one Cal Worthington. I recall Mr. Jones' paper because at first I thought he was creating a new Rorschach test. I gave him an A+ until I learned that the dark blots on his paper were grease marks. When I was finally able to uncover the actual content of the paper, I had to revise the grade to the more standard one of "A" which most of our students obtain here at California International.

On several occasions I had opportunity to interact with Mr. Jones off campus. I cannot remember all of the details, but at a student-faculty party at my personal residence the minority faculty in our department seemed to take umbrage at several witticisms which Mr. Jones felt compelled to relate late in the evening after he had, in all fairness to him, consumed a large number of Harvey Wallbangers and several rounds of a white material which he seemed to treat as snuff.

As compared with our other students, Mr. Jones was certainly high average (I would gather he was about 5'11" with his pumps on). He seemed to have the ability to bring mirth to a good number of people, what with the little beanie and propeller he wore around campus. I know our school nurse—since she had to monitor his medication—grew quite fond of Mr. Jones in those final months before her commitment.

If I can be of further assistance in your request for information, do not hesitate to call me at my office or at my home. As you are aware, much can be discussed over the phone which freedom of access makes rather difficult to commit to paper.

Sincerely and truly,

Larry Lister, D.S.W.
Professor and CEO

Figure 2. A sample letter of recommendation from a faculty member in response to a request by a student.

The Relationship Between Height, Intellectual Development, Speed of Thought, Appropriate Compensation for Faculty, and Related Matters

Harold M. Swartz, M.D., Ph.D.
University of Illinois College of Medicine at Urbana-Champaign

In the midst of interviewing an apparently good candidate (on paper) who was responding unsatisfactorily regarding his plans for pursuing a dual degree (M.D.-Ph.D.) career, the other committee members and I tried heroically to provide sufficient hints to inspire his answers. The student, however, made few and essentially irrelevant comments and remained steadfastly perplexed as to why anyone might pursue the path he proposed to follow. As he stood to go, nearly scraping the ceiling of our interview room, I achieved an important new insight into the process of thinking: the connection between height and intellectual capacity.

Generally, we consider that higher cognitive functions require communication between neurons, which are usually assumed to go from side-to-side. It became clear that in this individual, however, some of his key neuronal connections were arranged top-to-bottom and thus, unfortunately, had to travel via his unusually long spinal tract. Due to the necessity of sending information along this long tract not only were his thoughts being slowed down but, apparently, there was a significant probability of loss of phase and information. No wonder then that this poor fellow, who apparently had all the elements for an excellent career plan, couldn't really put it together.

As is the case in any inspirational leap forward in concepts, a number of other things immediately became obvious. His problem was only a singular manifestation of a general phenomenon: Some key cerebral neuronal connections always go via the spinal column! This explains why the intellectual giants and the sage politicians who really make a difference by virtue of their capabilities tend to be short (e.g., Mao, Napoleon, Deng, Tito, Thatcher, Truman, Gorbachev, not Reagan). While previous (erroneous) theories linking height and leadership have attributed the drive and ambition of short individuals to their attempts to overcome negative images associated with short stature, the truth was now apparent: These people are accomplishing more simply because they are superior. For those thought processes which need to go up and down the spinal column, short people have a natural advantage by having a shorter spinal column to traverse. As a consequence, their conclusions are inevitably less prone to error and, to boot, are reached more quickly.

I discussed these insights, at the conclusion of the interview, with the faculty member to my right. He immediately grasped the significance and implications of this finding and, drawing himself up to his full 5' 2" stature, emphatically agreed and in fact expounded on some useful extensions which I will discuss below. As in any important new idea, however, our conclusions did not go without reaching some opposition from entrenched, conventional, and one might even say, heightest thinkers. Our colleague at the end of the table, a faculty member known for his prowess as a basketball player before turning full time to more traditional academic pursuits, vigorously disagreed with our conclusions. It was obvious to us, however, that his body build unfortunately had given him less than a full deck with which to play and therefore we could safely ignore his protestations.

Instead of concerning ourselves with his ill-found objections, we considered how to exploit our newfound insights. In the competitive model which is now rampant in modern society, it was apparent that provisions need to be made to take into account the natural superiority of individuals with short spinal columns. We currently are drawing up a proposal to rearrange faculty pay scales to take into account this most significant variable. Henceforth, pay and promotion will depend inversely upon the length of the spinal column. This will provide immediate relief to our long-spinal-column brethren who no longer will have to suffer the anxiety and eventual disappointment from not receiving promotion and increased pay at the same rate as their better-endowed colleagues. Instead, their pay will be based on a different scale so that the lesser amounts they receive will be expected and thereby the lesser success will be in line with their talents as ordained by their height. They will no longer have to suffer guilt for appearing to have not tried their best and now will know that they are neuronally handicapped and are doing as well as is possible under the circumstances. We anticipate that the demeanor and actions of these colleagues will be improved by reducing their disappointments from unmet and indeed, now that we understand the situation, unfeasible expectations.

In the course of the discussions, as we were both scratching our beards, other correlates came to mind. The first correlate we discovered caused immediate shock: It implicitly supports the natural superiority of women! However, again using historical review, we were able to explain away this obviously false deduction: It is clear that most of the major discoveries have been made by short men with beards. Beardedness, we reasoned, is not a coincidence but again an example of cause and effect. Obviously, on the basis of a mechanism yet to be completely determined, the presence of facial hair enhances neuronal interconnections, perhaps even more than short stature, and certainly has a synergistic effect when combined with such stature. We therefore are modifying our plan for faculty compensation to include additional bonus points for those with the requisite length of beard. This will help offset the apparent advantage of height (i.e., lack of height) of women as well, a point we readily agreed upon.

I also noted, while straightening out my glasses on my well-endowed nose, that there are other characteristics that seem to be associated with high achievements of faculty. My colleague, whose glasses were precariously balanced on his rather small and inadequate nose, somehow failed to see the wisdom of this latest insight. As a friendly gesture, I have temporarily withdrawn the additional points related to the length of the external olfactory apparatus.

We were tempted, but declined, to extend these observations into further explanations pertaining to the two sexes. For example, it was proposed but at least temporarily rejected that there might be a correlation between more rounded body contours and the efficiency of side-to-side pathways. We felt that the data were inadequate to draw firm conclusions in this regard; we are awaiting future candidates to observe.

Figure 1. Illustration of some of the physical characteristics associated with superior intellectual capabilities.

It seems possible that we have not explored all of the anatomical features that may be related to the efficiency of neuronal pathways. I hope that readers of this article will reflect on their experience and knowledge and add to this rapidly growing area which, when perfected, should enable us to predict intellectual success much more accurately (see Figure 1) and thereby provide more prompt rewards for the deserving and more realistic expectations for those who are not ideally endowed.

A Quick Guide to Understanding Student Evaluations

Craig Bowman, Ph.D.
California State University at Fullerton

Student evaluations of courses and instructors are not, as is commonly assumed, meaningless, useless, or irrelevant. Such feedback needs to be properly interpreted. This is best accomplished by applying some basic psychological theories (e.g., perspective-taking) to the task of figuring out just what students are trying to convey to the instructor. For example, if students complain that a course is too difficult, this should not necessarily be seen as a negative comment. A more appropriate and positive interpretation would be that the students found themselves intellectually challenged.

Psychologists in academic settings are uniquely qualified to perform this task but, unfortunately, few have the time to figure out what the students are trying to say. For those readers with not enough time or imagination, the author presents here a few interpretations of commonly occurring student comments.

Comment	Interpretation
The course was a disappointment to me.	They told me this was an easy course.
The book is difficult to read.	The book needed more cartoons.
Assignments were too long for those of us with outside jobs.	I didn't have the time to waste doing the assignments because I'm vitally needed at work—the French fryer keeps breaking down.
You are the best instructor I've ever had.	I missed an A by one point and I was hoping. . . .

Comment	Interpretation
The lectures were highly structured.	Thanks for spelling those hard words on the board for us.
The tests were too hard.	Nobody told me I had to study to pass.
The tests were too easy.	. . . for someone of MY superior ability.
I learned a lot.	I missed a B by one point and I was hoping. . . .
You did a marvelous job of presenting many contrasting theories and ideas.	Thank God you didn't drone on and on about your own stupid research.
Assignments were not graded fairly.	Since this isn't an English course I don't think it's fair to take off for spelling.
I wish I had done better in your course.	Boy! Are Mom and Dad gonna freak when they see this grade!
I was not motivated to do my best.	Clearly it is YOUR fault I'm flunking.
The instructor needs to add humor to his lectures.	Not one sex or drug joke the whole time!
You should encourage more classroom participation.	Just what is so wrong about talking to my friends during your lectures?
My grade does not reflect what I have learned in this course.	I missed a passing grade by one point and I was hoping. . . .

The Academic Oedipal Crisis:
An Experimental Investigation of
the Need of Assistant Professors
to Kill Their Departmental Chairman

David L. Coulter, M.D.
Boston University School of Medicine

There comes a time in the career of most assistant professors (usually during their fifth or sixth year in rank) when it becomes necessary to consider how to kill their departmental chairman. This often happens because of some arbitrary, irrational, and capricious administrative action that infringes on the assistant professor's developing sense of mastery. In view of these facts and the relative excess of assistant professors, it is surprising how few chairmen are actually murdered. Thinking about it may be more important than actually doing it, however, and considering how to murder one's chairman may be a predictable stage of academic career development. Alternatively, assistant professors may simply lack sufficient creativity, since the literature offers no guidance in this area. In an effort to stimulate further work in this area, the author explores in the present study underlying developmental issues related to the urge of assistant professors to kill their departmental chairman and identifies specific methods that can be utilized to bring about sudden academic career opportunities.

Theory

It is well known (Sophocles, 450 B.C.) that Oedipus killed his father in order to assume his father's role as a husband to his mother. More recently (Freud, 1960), it has been recognized that all male children harbor oedipal feelings of homicidal intent toward their fathers during an early stage of psychosexual development. Male children ultimately resolve the oedipal situation by becoming fathers themselves. This provides an insight into the oedipal nature of academic career development.

Assistant professors begin their careers by assuming a filial relationship to their departmental chairman. As the assistant professors develop, they see their chairman as a model of what they want to be. In order to take over the chairman's role, however, they believe the chairman must be killed like Oedipus killed his father. According to this theory, assistant professors want to kill their chairman so that they can become chairman themselves. Indeed, it may be stated that chairmen have a duty to die (Lamm, 1983) so that assistant professors can grow and develop normally.

The neurotic implications of the process are evident, since the assistant professor regresses to a cognitive stage of egocentricity and preoperational thought (Piaget, 1969). This regression causes the assistant professor to forget how to become a chairman. Specifically, he ignores the need for growth through the stage of associate professor and full professor, neurotically thinking that he can become chairman as soon as the real chairman dies. Therapeutically, it should be apparent that promotion to associate professor would eliminate the regression and effectively solve the academic oedipal crisis. Since the author has not yet reached the stage of associate professor, these issues will be considered in future studies. A career development award has been requested to support this research.

It is unclear whether the theory also applies to female assistant professors with male chairmen. Furthermore, the theory does not predict the behavior of male assistant professors with female chairmen, nor does it specify the developmental role of female chairmen in the careers of their male assistant professors. Female assistant professors with female chairpersons might want to kill them as part of an academic Electra crisis, but this needs further study. The author's wife has requested grant support from the Women's Auxiliary of the American Psychoanalytic Association to pursue this area of research.

Hypothesis

This study sought first to explore in a preliminary way how assistant professors want to kill their chairman. It was hypothesized that assistant professors would not lack creativity but might lack the opportunity. Thus, the second issue tested was that assistant professors whose chairman had been removed might think differently about murder. The hypothesis that all male assistant professors undergo an academic oedipal crisis was explored to test the developmental theory outlined above.

Method

It is acknowledged that there may be "Fifty ways to leave your lover" (Simon, 1981), but the number of ways to kill one's chairman is likely more finite. This study compared homicidal thinking in two groups of assistant professors. Group A consisted of five assistant professors whose male chairman was still alive and seated, while Group B consisted of five assistant professors whose male chairman had recently retired, suffered a heart attack, died, or been fired by the dean. All study subjects were male and had been in rank at least 5, but not more than 7, years. Each subject was interviewed at length in private, using as much alcohol as necessary to obtain valid results. No attempt was made to inform the subjects' chairmen of the results, since this would have confounded subsequent analysis of outcome. Since this was conceptualized as a psychoanalytic study, no statistical analysis was felt to be necessary.

Results

The results are presented in Table 1. While there was no real difference between Group A and Group B, it was apparent that both groups preferred violent, painful methods, so long as the results were the same (death).

Table 1. How to Kill Your Chairman

Method	Group A	Group B
Gunfire	3	3
("Blow him away," or "C'mon punk, make my day!")		
Slaughter	0	1
("I wish he were an Oscar Meyer wiener")		
Lynching	1	1
("Hang 'em high")		
Bizarre	1*	0
("Kill, Jason, Kill!")		

*This subject was excluded from further analysis (see Results).

One subject was excluded from the study because he wanted to split his chairman's skull with an axe at camp or behead him with a chainsaw in Texas. This subject frequently watched cable-TV horror movies at night instead of writing grant proposals.

All subjects agreed on the need to kill their chairman. The most common reasons given were arbitrary and unreasonable restrictions on research time, insufficient laboratory space, excessive teaching demands, inadequate secretarial support, and low salaries (in that order). Subjects in clinical departments also mentioned the need to generate revenues to support nonproductive senior professors who sat in their offices all day. Several subjects also noted that their chairman didn't let them attend enough professional meetings.

Each subject was asked specifically whether he wanted to become a chairman. All said, Yes. Six thought they were ready now, and two commented that they already had more grants and publications than their chairman.

Discussion

It was apparent that assistant professors do not lack for creativity when considering how to kill their chairman. In fact, on some occasions the author felt overwhelmed by the intensity of these disclosures; only the privileged and protected nature of the experimenter-subject relationship prevented him from disclosing some of these communications to the authorities. The similarity between Group A and Group B responses suggests that opportunity was not a factor, and that reality testing is not necessary when considering how to kill one's chairman. This supports the regressive psychodynamic aspect of the theory as described above.

The interviews indicated that each assistant professor wanted to kill his chairman and each wanted to become a chairman himself. These results validate the theory of a developmental academic oedipal crisis. Current departmental chairmen may draw two conclusions from this study: retire now, or promote your assistant professors as soon as possible.

It should be noted that, according to the theory, promoting an assistant professor effectively resolves his academic oedipal crisis. It is not known, however, whether tenured associate professors also want to replace their chairman. Until further research is done in this area, current chairmen should also be wary of their tenured faculty. Chairmen who do not plan to retire may wish to help their tenured faculty obtain chairmanships elsewhere.

References

Freud, S. (1960). *A general introduction to psychoanalysis.* New York: Washington Square Press.

Lamm, R. (1983). Published remarks by the Governor of Colorado.

Piaget, J., & Inhelder, B. (1969). *The psychology of the child.* New York: Basic Books.

Simon, P. (1981). *Fifty ways to leave your lover.* Overheard on the radio.

Sophocles. (450 B.C.). *Oedipus Rex.* Athens: Academy Press.

Reviewerese: A Brief Glossary of Remarks Commonly Appearing in Reviews of Articles Submitted for Publication in Psychological Journals

John B. Pittenger, Ph.D., and Paul Whitney, Ph.D.
University of Arkansas at Little Rock

While many writers have discussed the nature of the written dialect known as "journalese," the jargon of journal editors and reviewers has been neglected. Psychologists who are inexperienced in the art of journal publication may be unaware of the subtle nuances of the argot of peer review. Accordingly, we have listed a number of the common circumlocutions along with their translation into ordinary English.

The reader should, however, take note of two cautions. First, some editors and reviewers say exactly what they mean. Thus, care must be taken in deciding whether to translate feedback from the review process. A useful rule of thumb is that reviews containing many long involuted sentences are typically of the jargon sort. Second, we are not concerned here with comments made by reviewers who completely miss the point of the paper. Such reviews are known technically as "Bozo" reviews. While sometimes it seems that the number of non-Bozo reviews is amazingly small, there is a developmental progression in one's reaction to a review in that some reviews become less Bozo the more we think about them (see Underwood, 1957).[1] Thus, in the present paper we concentrate on comments

---

[1] It may be noted in passing that Bozo reviewers can often be bamboozled with either of two strategies: (1) cite everything you've ever published whether it's relevant or not so you'll appear to be an unimpeachable expert, or (2) come up with a very catchy name for your theoretical constructs. A danger of these strategies is, of course, they may cause non-Bozo reviewers to cream you.

made by those who more or less understand the author's work but seem intent on making their criticism oblique.

I. Comments Made by Reviewers

What the reviewer writes	What the reviewer means
1. The author seems unaware of much of the literature relevant to this topic. For example, Jones' well-known 1978 study is not mentioned.	1. I'm Jones and I'm miffed.
2. The author presents, and then shoots down, only a "straw man" version of Jones' theory.	2. I'm Jones and I'm *very* miffed.
3. The statistical analyses of the results a. are overly elaborate and involuted. b. use obscure tests not likely to be known to the average reader.	3. The statistical analyses of the results a. confuse me. b. were new to me and I had to look them up.
4. The author, when presenting her discussion of the results a. grossly overgeneralizes the theoretical implications. b. shows great insight into the implications of this research. c. ignores some of the more subtle points made by the data.	4. The author, when presenting her discussion of the results a. comes to a conclusion incompatible with my theoretical bias. b. comes to a conclusion compatible with my theoretical bias. c. could have come to a conclusion compatible with my theory and cited me, but she didn't.
5. Although these experiments have a solid design and the results are clean, the overall contribution of this study is too low to warrant publication.	5. This is good research on an idea I don't like. There is no concrete problem with it but I would just as soon ignore it.
6. To be certain that my objections are not due to any personal bias on my part, I showed the paper to several colleagues. They all shared my reservations.	6. My graduate students didn't like it either.

What the reviewer writes	What the reviewer means
7. The development of the theoretical background is a. long and rambling.	7. The development of the theoretical background a. mentions several obviously wrong-headed theories.
b. long, rambling, unclear, and argumentative.	b. supports a stupid theory and attacks my theory.
c. long, rambling, unclear, argumentative, and dwells on picky, arcane theoretical points.	c. attacks my theory and digs up skeletons that should remain buried.
8. The author introduces a novel theoretical approach and has employed innovative methods. However, neither the ideas nor the methods are sufficiently well developed to warrant publication at this time.	8. *Caution: This remark is ambiguous.* It can mean either: a. This stuff is too weird for words. b. This guy's ideas are dangerous and need to be nipped in the bud.
9. While the author uses a trendy theoretical approach, the actual substance of the article hardly warrants publication.	9. These weird ideas are getting more and more popular. If we don't stop them soon, they are going to take over.

[Years pass. The authors become the reviewers and recent graduates start submitting papers.]

10. While purporting to adhere to the tenets of the dominant theory, the author actually deeply misunderstands its core concepts.	10. I don't believe it! We've finally taken over this journal and now a bunch of revisionist kids are stirring everything up again.

II. The Journal Editor's Remarks

What the editor writes	What the editor means
1. The three reviewers came to somewhat different conclusions.	1. One person loved it, one hated it, and the third found it merely dull.
2. Should you choose to rewrite and resubmit your paper, please enclose a cover letter detailing how you dealt with the objections made by reviewer B.	2. I can't figure out what reviewer B means but the objections sound serious. You might as well figure it out because if reviewer B obsessed on those points so will somebody else.

What the editor writes	What the editor means
3. Please excuse the long delay in coming to a decision on your paper. As you know we receive many submissions and take great care. . . .	3. Oops. I just found your manuscript under a pile of ungraded undergraduate essays.
4. My delay in reaching a decision on your manuscript was due to the fact that the reviewers and I engaged in numerous discussions of your ideas.	4. It took two letters and five phone calls to get these wretches to send in their reviews.
5. While the contributions made in your research do not warrant publication in this journal, I do recommend that you submit it to the *Journal of [name deleted]*.	5. This work isn't very good but try the *Journal of [name deleted]*.
a. That journal, while of high quality, is able to publish work somewhat less definitive than we require.	a. They'll publish anything.
b. That journal does not suffer from the high rejection rate that we do.	b. Nobody sends anything to them any more and they'll be glad to get your stuff.
c. That journal will be eager to publish your paper.	c. That journal will be glad to accept your paper as long as you pay them $40 per page.
6. While this work does have points of interest, it is not sufficiently developed to warrant publication. If you pursue the work with more adequate methods I would be happy to consider. . . .	6. Go away and do it right next time.
7. This work is not sufficiently developed to warrant publication.	7. Just go away.
8. The serious defects in methodology, confusions in theoretical analyses, errors in statistics, . . .	8. Have you considered another career?

Reference

Underwood, B. J. (1957). *Psychological research*. New York: Appleton-Century-Crofts.

8
Experimental Psychology

An Overview of Research Findings in the Behavioral Sciences: The Laws of Psychology

Lawrence G. Calhoun, Ph.D., Arnie Cann, Ph.D., and W. Scott Terry, Ph.D.
University of North Carolina at Charlotte

While psychology can trace its historical roots to ancient Greek philosophers (Scott-Terry, 1986), the scientific and experimental basis of psychology was not laid down until the late 19th and early 20th centuries. Since those humble beginnings, scientific psychology has discovered important truths about human and animal nature. While much information on the major discoveries of psychology is readily available in such erudite sources as introductory psychology texts, these usually are very long. The average textbook has about 531 pages (Toner, 1986), not counting student guides, teacher manuals, transparencies, slides, software, and kickbacks. What is needed is a brief, concise statement of the laws of psychology that can serve as a ready reference for the scientist and the practitioner, and which can be distributed to the physician's waiting room.

The purpose of the present paper is to provide an accurate and concise summary of the important discoveries in the major areas of psychology. The laws were chosen based on their empirical history, the scientific nature of the research supporting them, and, most importantly, our own personal opinions. Laws for different areas of psychology will be listed separately.

Laws of Conditioning

Never sound a tone when one of Pavlov's dogs is sitting in your lap.
Never give a rabbit to a child named Albert.

The Four Laws of Memory

Whatever you think you remember, you probably don't.
Whatever you think you forgot, you probably didn't.
You are more likely to remember something if you don't forget it.
The fourth law is . . . ah . . . oh . . . it's on the tip of my tongue . . . I knew it a minute ago . . .

Laws of Behavior Modification

If you pay somebody to do something, he/she will probably do it again and demand money the next time he/she does.
People do what they like.
A reinforcer is whatever works.

Laws of Developmental Psychology

In general, young children tend to get older.
Adults get older faster than children, and adults *with* children get older the fastest.
Children only hear what they want to.
The Laws of Behavior Modification only apply to other people's children.

Laws of Clinical Psychology

Adolescence *is* a disease.
Only sick people can be cured.
Problems worth curing can be discussed in 50-minute blocks of time.

Laws of Sensation and Perception

Loud sounds always originate nearby.

Smaller objects tend to be farther away.

Object permanence—most objects are permanent, but you can never find the ones that are missing.

Laws of Industrial Psychology

Most people like their jobs, but hate work.

Employees who get more money tend to believe they have higher salaries.

Accidents happen.

Laws of Social Psychology

People who wear hoods cannot be trusted to give electric shock in a fair and impartial manner.

Do unto others only if you are pretty sure you won't be observed.

You can't violate someone's personal space without violating your own.

It's not who does it that's important—it's who gets blamed.

Laws of History and Systems of Psychology

Those who repeat the past will be doomed—unless they develop new linguistic patterns to describe the same old stuff.

Psychology has a long past, but only a short history (—Ebbinghaus); "History of Psychology" textbooks are longer than both of those combined (—student).

Laws of Community Psychology

An ounce of prevention is worth more than a pound of cure, but it weighs less.

Laws of Physiological Psychology

The brain of a dead animal is easier to work with.
Pain usually hurts.
The right hand *does* know what the left hand is doing—it just
doesn't care.
Blood is thicker than water and much harder to clean up.

Laws of Parapsychology

If they apply, you don't need to be told.

References

Scott-Terry, S. T. (1986). *Handbook of the history of psychology and organic gardening.*
Newell, NC: Ditto Press.
Toner, N. (1986). Practical applications of delay of gratification research:
How to wait until the intro books get longer. *Journal de la International
Exchange des Idées, 0,* 1–2.

Bright Light Therapy for the Treatment of Winter Depression: New Perspectives

Colin D. Field, M.Sc.
Institute for Iatrogenic Intervention
Adelaide, Australia

Researchers (Rosenthal, Sack, & Wehr, 1983) have recently noted a relationship between seasonal changes and the incidence of depression, coining the term Seasonal Affective Disorder (SAD). Rosenthal, Sack, Carpenter, Parry, Mendleson, and Wehr (1985) have hypothesized that SAD is associated with abnormally high rates of melatonin secretion in the brain. Reasoning that secretion of this hormone is related to length of daylight and illumination levels, several studies (Byerley, Brown, & Lebegue, 1987; Isaacs, Stainer, Sensky, Moor, & Thompson, 1988; Rosenthal et al., 1984) have demonstrated that exposing endogenously depressed patients to simulated sunlight results in the amelioration of depressive symptoms.

Some of the research boys at the Institute for Iatrogenic Intervention have been working on replicating this research. Unfortunately, recent funding cuts here meant that we were unable to afford the equipment specified by Rosenthal et al. (1984). Our resourceful staff could not however be dissuaded from pioneering some new inroads into this burgeoning area of treatment for depression. Their findings are reported below.

Experiment 1: Does Extra Light Improve Depression?

Method

Subjects

Candidate subjects were depressed, and clinical interview failed to demonstrate any valid reason for their depression. On this basis they were diagnosed as endogenously depressed (*endo* = I can't find; *geno* = a better reason). Four subjects were inpatients at the Institute. The remaining 16 were staff members. It was felt that these represented a homogeneous group.

All candidate subjects were removed from antidepressant medication 2 weeks before the scheduled start of the experiment. All surviving candidates (those who had not fulfilled the Spontaneous Suicide criterion) were randomly assigned to the experimental and control groups ($n = 2$ for each group).

Procedure

Subjects' depression was self-rated on a 2-point scale (1 = depressed; 2 = feeling better) before the beginning of the first session, and once again after the end of the last session.

Subjects were placed in an empty 10 ft. × 10 ft. × 10 ft. room with a 150-W light bulb mounted in the ceiling, for four sessions of 4 hours each. Subjects in the control group were placed in the room with the light bulb operated in the "off" mode (i.e., with the experimenter-controlled switch in the "off" position). Subjects in the experimental group were placed in the room with the light bulb operated in the "on" mode (i.e., with the experimenter-controlled switch in the "on" position).

Results

Results were disappointing. By the time the experiment started, all four surviving subjects were rating themselves as "2 = feeling better." Nevertheless, the experiment carried on.

Following completion of the sessions, one control subject still rated himself as "2 = feeling better," while the other not only rated himself as depressed, but also added a "3 = scared of the dark" comment on his rating sheet.

Both of the experimental subjects rated themselves as "1 = depressed" following the end of the experimental manipulation. The first added that he was now also bored. The second commented that he wished that the light cord had been longer, so that he could have reached up and put his finger in the socket. Both of these subjects were employees of the Institute, and subsequently had their employment terminated for conspiring to falsify experimental data.

Experiment 2: While the Subjects Are Sitting in There, What Else Can We Get Them to Do?

When one of the experimental subjects in Experiment 1 commented that he was bored, this set our research team thinking. When we finished thinking, we ran a second, redesigned experiment, described below.

Method

Four surviving candidate subjects, selected in the same way as described in Experiment 1, were randomly assigned to experimental and control groups. This time all candidates were staff members, as it was felt that the ability to terminate the employment of outlying data points was a worthwhile innovation.

Subjects' depression levels were rated on the 2-point scale described in Experiment 1.

All subjects were placed in an empty 10 ft. $\times$ 10 ft. $\times$ 10 ft. room, with a lighted 150-W light bulb mounted in the ceiling, for four sessions of 4 hours each. Subjects in the control group were placed in the room with the light bulb operated in the "on" mode (i.e., the same as for the *experimental* group in Experiment 1). During the sessions they were given serial presentations of The Self-Fulfilling Prophecy Depression Scale (Field, 1988a, 1988b), a new self-administered depression rating scale which is replete with questions like, "If you're so damned depressed, why don't you off yourself right now?"

It was felt that this was also a worthwhile innovation, as it ensured that control subjects would not spontaneously recover from their depression half-way through the experiment.

Subjects in the experimental group were placed in a lighted room with a deck chair, an umbrella, a pair of sunglasses, a bottle of suntan lotion, a liberal supply of glossy magazines, and a crate of cheap champagne left over from the Institute's Christmas party.

Results

This time, results were equivocal. At the outset, the two control and the two experimental subjects rated themselves as "1 = depressed."

Following the experimental manipulation, one control subject still rated himself as "1 = depressed," and had his contract renewed as a consequence. The second rated himself as "2 = feeling better," and added that he thought the test-retest reliability for The Self-Fulfilling Prophecy Depression Scale (which he had calculated during the boring moments) "stinks." As a consequence, his employment at the Institute was terminated.

The first member of the experimental group once again rated himself as "1 = depressed," and also added that "it was a dirty trick to offer me that rotten champagne again when everyone at the Christmas party had stayed away from it; at least you could have put the corks back in." Of course, his employment was terminated. The second member of the experimental group rated himself as "2 = feeling better," adding that he had a nice time, and is therefore still working for the people who pay his salary.

Experiment 3: What's So Good about Summer Sunlight, Anyway?

The research team thought some more. We thought to ourselves, What's so good about summer sunlight, anyway? After all, you can get sunburnt. What's so good about going to the beach? Who wants gritty sand between their toes? Who wants melted ice creams dripping through their fingers? Who wants to be bitten by sandflies and sharks? Who wants to stare at some dopey bright light anyhow?

Naturally, these questions led us to investigate the effect of winter lighting conditions on depressed patients.

Method

Four surviving candidate subjects, selected in the same way as described in Experiment 1, were randomly assigned to experimental and control groups. Once again, all candidates were staff members. Subjects' depression levels were again rated on the 2-point scale described in Experiment 1.

Once again, subjects were placed in an empty 10 ft. × 10 ft. × 10 ft. room, with an operating 150-W light bulb mounted in the ceiling, for four sessions of 4 hours each.

Subjects in the control group were placed in the room with a deck chair, an umbrella, a pair of sunglasses, a bottle of suntan lotion, a liberal supply of glossy magazines, a crate of cheap champagne left over from the Institute's Christmas party, gritty sand on the floor, melted ice creams dripping through their fingers, and several sandflies and small sharks.

Subjects in the experimental group were placed in the room with a deck chair, an umbrella, a pair of warm boots, an overcoat, a scarf, a liberal supply of glossy magazines, a crate of cold beer, a television set tuned to the local football game, and a vendor selling meat pies.[1]

Results

Results were most satisfactory. Once again, at the outset, the two control and two experimental subjects rated themselves as "1 = depressed."

Following the experimental manipulation, both control subjects still rated themselves as "1 = depressed." Both had been bitten by sandflies, and one, in a small way, by a shark. Both subjects are now on sick leave from the Institute.

Both members of the experimental group rated themselves as

---

[1] A local Australian delicacy. U.S. investigators wanting to replicate this experiment may substitute a hot dog stand if they wish.

"2 = feeling better," although one expressed a desire to watch a first-run game on television, rather than last week's repeat. The other spontaneously commented, "It's a pity it didn't rain."

Discussion

It is clear from the three experiments reported that boredom, as well as lighting levels, plays a role in the presentation of the seasonally depressed patient. It appears that there is not only a group of depressed patients that gets more depressed in winter due to reduced lighting levels (which we now refer to as "Type I seasonals"), but also a hitherto unreported summer seasonal depressive subgroup ("Type II seasonals").

We thought we could probably get some more mileage out of this concept, but we've just had our grant revoked, because of what were referred to as "confounded variables." That's what we thought about the variables too.

References

Byerley, W. F., Brown, J.-A., & Lebegue, B. (1987). Treatment of seasonal affective disorder with morning light. *Journal of Clinical Psychiatry, 48,* 447–448.

Field, C. D. (1988a). *The Self-Fulfilling Prophecy Depression Scale: If you're not depressed now, you will be by the time you fill this out.* Unpublished manuscript, The Institute for Iatrogenic Intervention.

Field, C. D. (1988b). *The Self-Fulfilling Prophecy Depression Scale: How to create new depressed patients when you can't get your hands on old ones.* Unpublished manuscript, The Institute for Iatrogenic Intervention.

Isaacs, G., Stainer, D. S., Sensky, T. E., Moor, S., & Thompson, C. (1988). Phototherapy and its mechanisms in seasonal affective disorder. *Journal of Affective Disorders, 14,* 13–19.

Rosenthal, N. E., Sack, D. A., Carpenter, C. J., Parry, B. L., Mendleson, W. B., & Wehr, T. A. (1985). Antidepressant effect of light in seasonal affective disorder. *American Journal of Psychiatry, 142,* 163–170.

Rosenthal, N. E., Sack, D. A., Gillin, J. C., Lewy, A. J., Goodwin, F. K., Davenport, Y., Mueller, P. S., Newsome, D. A., & Wehr, T. A. (1984). Seasonal affective disorder. A description of the syndrome and preliminary findings with light therapy. *Archives of General Psychiatry, 41,* 72–80.

Rosenthal, N. E., Sack, D. A., & Wehr, T. A. (1983). Seasonal variations in affective disorder. In T. A. Wehr & F. K. Goodwin (Eds.), *Circadian rhythms in psychiatry* (pp. 185–202). Los Angeles: Boxwood.

9
Statistics

A Beginner's Guide to
Statistical Terms in
the Psychological Literature

Alan Feingold, Ed.M.
Yale University

Novice researchers and those other than social scientists oftentimes find the psychological literature intimidating due to the abundance of statistical terms found in psychology journals. To make matters worse, many of these terms have completely different meanings in the psychological literature than they do in everyday life, evoking considerable confusion among statistically unsophisticated readers. In order to help those unfamiliar with psychological statistics to master the basics, the author highlights here 20 potential sources of confusion involving statistical terminology frequently used in psychology.

1. A *t* test does not determine how many people prefer Lipton's. The *F* test does not reveal who is "good in bed." And the runs test does not evaluate the effect of Mexican food on biological functioning.

2. A statistical interaction should never be confused with a social interaction. The latter makes life more pleasant. The former makes life less pleasant. Also, a "three-way interaction" has an entirely different meaning in ANOVA than it does in an X-rated video.

3. The "familywise error rate" denotes the probability of making an erroneous statistical decision. It has nothing to do with the frequency of mistakes made by mom, dad, and the kids.

4. Citations to "Kirk" probably refer to a statistical text and not to the commander of the *U.S.S. Enterprise.*

5. "Multicollinearity" is not a life-threatening condition, except when a depressed graduate student's thesis employs many redundant measures.

6. When the null hypothesis gets rejected, it does not feel upset or discouraged.

7. Meteorologists do not use principal components analysis to get the wind-chill factor.

8. Statistical power does not corrupt, except when a finding comes out strongly in the "wrong" direction and a one-tailed test suddenly becomes a two-tailed test.

9. A "mean square" is a type of variance, not a nasty person who isn't hip.

10. Bivariate relationships do not promote the spread of AIDS.

11. "H_0" denotes the null hypothesis, not what Santa Claus yells three times on Christmas Eve.

12. It's important to distinguish between a "causal model" and a "casual model." A causal model is a predicted pattern of intercorrelations. (A casual model is a pretty girl who earns money by being photographed in her spare time.) When it is noted that a causal model is able to be "identified," it does not mean that a witness pointed at it and exclaimed, "That's it! That's the one! I'd know it anywhere."

13. The harmonic mean is not more melodious than the arithmetic mean.

14. When factors are "fixed," it's not because they were broken.

15. It is not sexist to use the term "MANOVA," although some feminists prefer "PERSONOVA."

16. The terms "mean" and "median" refer to preferred measures of central tendency, except when the variable is ice cream. (One does not speak of "pie à la mean" or "pie à la median.")

17. When a statistician says "μ," he/she is talking about the mean of a population, and not the sound made by a cow.

18. The term "heteroscedasticity" was not invented by therapists to assess speech impediments. (Whether it can serve that purpose, however, is another matter.)

19. A "package" is a computer program. (And anyone who's seen the SAS documentation knows that good things do *not* come in small packages.) Also, BMDP should not be confused with BMW. The critical difference is that psychologists, sociologists, and epide-

miologists run BMDP, whereas lawyers, doctors, and executives run BMWs.

20. Random sampling in psychology refers to nonsystematic selection from a well-defined universe, such as all freshmen at a given college who sign up for an experiment for money, credit, or "just for the hell of it."

A Significantly Significant Approach to Significant Research Findings: The Salzman All-Significant *F* Test

Kenneth L. Salzman, Ph.D.

The field of psychology has long been hampered rather than helped by the statistical procedures available to the average researcher. The resulting confusion, frustration, and depression have impeded the progress of our science and resulted in untold suffering among its practitioners. The Salzman All-Significant *F* Test was developed to meet the needs of the psychology research community and to resolve the problems inherent in reality based statistical methods.

Since its beginning, research in the social sciences has been obstructed by the existence of complex, convoluted, and incomprehensible statistical procedures (Veysmeer, 1982). The statistical approaches available today continue to beleaguer social scientists by too frequently producing nonsignificant results. The lack of reliable statistical procedures (that is to say, procedures which would give reliably supportive results) has led to the inhibition of whole lines of theoretical inquiry (Ether, 1956; Phlogistan, 1937; Skenner, 1983). This kind of wholesale rejection of brilliant concepts and theories has prematurely terminated many otherwise promising careers. It has been shown that these researchers would have gone on to become major players in the social sciences, drawing large incomes and significantly contributing to the national tax base (Salzman, 1985).

Students are perhaps the most severely plagued by the current state of the art in statistical science. Advanced students in the social sciences experience a nearly phobic response to the need to use, let alone understand, statistical techniques (Nocomps, 1981; Nostats, 1976; Nosweat, 1985). Their progress toward degree acquisition and earning potential is severely delayed. This penalty is exacted from these students with no concern for their dedication to the field and with total disregard for their skills, abilities, and interests. This hardship is perhaps felt most deeply by clinical psychology students, who don't really want to do the research anyway (Rubin, 1986).

It is with these concerns in mind that the Salzman All-Significant F Test was developed. The Salzman All-Significant F Test resolves all the former difficulties experienced by researchers in the social sciences, forever removing the stigma of invalidated research and failed theories. Developed by a clinician with strong quantitative leanings, the Salzman All-Significant F Test is offered as a means of bringing about a renaissance in social sciences research and establishing forever the economic security of its creator.

Method of Use

The Salzman All-Significant F Test can be used on any MSDOS-compatible computer. While a color graphics capability is not required, the lack of such makes truly colorful results difficult to achieve. In addition to these basic requirements, the following are recommended:

- Two disk drives for two-tailed tests
- Hard disk drive for hard research
- Dot matrix printer for printing a correlation matrix
- High-resolution monitor for those intending to finish on schedule

The Salzman All-Significant F Test follows the latest recommendations for maximal user friendliness (Rogers, 1984). After the initial welcoming screen and accompanying song, the routine recommends that the user gets some milk and cookies before continuing. After the snack, the user is prompted to enter the degrees of freedom for their dataset.

In our extensive Beta-testing (Beta, 1985), we discovered that many users are somewhat unsure about their degrees of freedom. After considerable research (Falwell, 1981; Lear, 1981), we decided that the anxieties over this concern warranted the addition of an optional routine which randomly selects degrees of freedom for this uncertain user. If anything, research suggests that this has improved the effectiveness of the procedure (Salzman, 1985).

Once the degrees of freedom are chosen, the user proceeds to enter data. Data entry is free form and unstructured, allowing the user to enter data any way he/she wishes. Building on the work of Cann, Calhoun, Toner, Long, and Hagan (1985) and Scott-Terry (1942), the Salzman All-Significant F Test is capable of operating in Ultimate Stage Non-Data Mode, that is, without any data at all. Some researchers, however, may feel uncomfortable with this power. To assuage their unease, we recommend that they enter data from their dataset until such time as they no longer feel guilty about not having worked hard enough on the statistical analysis. (It should be noted that some users continue to feel concerned even after entering their entire dataset. For these miserable souls, we suggest that they replicate their data by entering it all again and/or seek counseling.)

System Output

The Salzman All-Significant F Test provides a full-screen graphic display (see Figure 1) which can be printed out if desired for inclusion in the research report. This display is guaranteed to provide maximum complexity, ensuring that readers of the report will decline to examine it and approve the research on the belief that there must be some significance contained within. The effectiveness of this procedure has been empirically confirmed (Snow, 1979).

Having entered the data and selected the desired figures, the user is then treated to a heartening display of blinking lights, disk drives running, and machine noises. After a satisfying period of time, the Salzman All-Significant F Test presents the user with an F statistic, guaranteed to be significant. Unlike the current methods available, where the significance levels are set at the whim of the statistical procedures, the Salzman All-Significant F Test gives the user control over the level of significance desired. The levels of signifi-

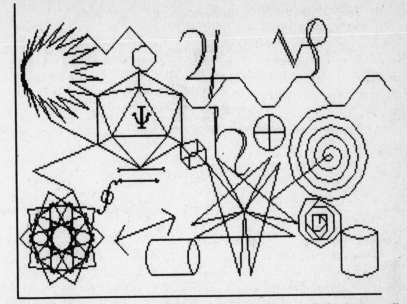

Figure 1. Representative examples of the flexibility of the Salzman All-Significant F Test graphics in generating a difficult-to-interpret figure.

cance available are shown in Table 1. Regardless of the level chosen, the F statistic provided is given to 14 decimal digits for maximal precision and effect.

Discussion

Thanks to the development of the Salzman All-Significant F Test, we are confident that there will no longer be the frustration of watching one's efforts come to naught due to lack of statistical significance in the data. No more will researchers have to discard their favored theoretical concepts. Now, the entire field of psychology can move forward, unimpeded by the chains of limiting statistical procedures. It is with great humility, and some avarice, that the author makes this boon available to all. And, for those who respond right now, we will add, absolutely free (while supplies last), the Ginzu Shredder used to obliterate the original raw data and thus avoid the embarrassment of evaluation by unenlightened colleagues. Order NOW!

Table 1. The Salzman All-Significant F Test Versions, Significance Levels, and Price

Version	Significance levels	Price
1.0	Significant at the .05 level	$ 14.95
2.0	Significant at the .01 level	$ 24.95
3.0	Significant at the .001 level	$129.95

Note. Version 3.0 is recommended for use with grants.

References

Beta, U. (1985). Evaluations of computer applications. *Tests and Measurements Weekly, 14,* 17–23.

Cann, A., Calhoun, L., Toner, I., Long, G., & Hagan, M. (1985). The issue of no-show subjects: A failure to replicate non-data on non-volunteer no-shows. *Journal of Polymorphous Perversity, 2*(1), 3–5.

Ether, N. (1956). Toward a new understanding of light transmission. *New Breakthroughs in Science Weekly, 1,* 1–16.

Falwell, J. (1981). In the way of American freedom. *Journal of Ways for the American People, 2,* 1980–1988.

Lear, N. (1981). Freedom in the American way. *Journal of People for the American Way, 2,* 18–29.

Nocomps, Z. Erehed Nostat. (1981) Computer consultants can be useful spouses. *Lonely Hearts Quarterly, 11,* 2–5.

Nostats, Z. Erehed. (1976). Statisticians can be useful spouses. *Lonely Hearts Quarterly, 6,* 2–5.

Nosweat, Z. Erehed Nostat Nocomp. (1985). Full professors can be useful spouses: The acquisition of a doctorate. *Lonely Hearts Quarterly, 15,* 2–5.

Phlogistan, Ari. (1937). Toward a new understanding of fire. *Breakthroughs in Science Weekly, 1,* 1–16.

Rogers, Mister. (1984). Hi there neighbor! *Journal of Saccharine Applications, 12,* 22.

Rubin, D. (1986). Surviving the graduate program. *Journal of Innovative Politics, 25,* 12–27.

Salzman, K. (1985). Applications of the Salzman All-Significant F Test, Part 1. *Journal of Unpublished Manuscripts, 8,* 1–286.

Scott-Terry, S. (1942). The fudge factor in the ultimate stage. *Journal of Psychic Nonreality, 3,* 3–33.

Skenner, S. (1983). Toward a new understanding of behavior. *Modern Breakthroughs in Science Weekly, 1,* 1–16.

Snow, C. (1979). Research jobs. *Journal of Self-Aggrandizement, 49,* 890–956.

Veysmeer, Oy. (1982). Mishugas in statistical research. *Roof Fiddlers Quarterly, 64,* 654–666.

10

Psychology Journal and Book Club Advertisements

Coming in Spring 1989...

The

Journal

of

Euthanasia:

Theory, Research, and Practice

BOARD OF DIRECTORS[1]

James C. Alt, M.D.
Deceased

Cynthia Block, M.D.
Deceased

Jay L. Fernly, Psy.D.
Deceased

Nigel R. Harrison, J.D.
Deceased

Stanly Smith, M.A.
Deceased

Ruth A. Stern, Ph.D.
Deceased

William Totwell, Th.D.
Deceased

Administrative Assistant

Mary Schneider

[1]Because of an unusually high turn-over rate among board members, many positions on the Board of Directors are now open. Applicants should submit their applications ATTN: Mary Schneider, Administrative Assistant.

The American Hemlockian Association is pleased to announce the publication of **The Journal of Euthanasia: Theory, Research, and Practice**, the official periodical of the AHA. While the number of issues per volume is still undecided, each issue will present scholarly articles of singular clarity and focus on the theory, research, and practice of euthanasia. Members of the Board of Directors of the American Hemlockian Association, each a world renowned expert on the topic of euthanasia, will serve as editors of **The Journal of Euthanasia**. Submissions of highly relevant theoretical and practical articles relating to the topic of euthanasia are invited from the research and clinical community.

1-year subscriptions (domestic): $54.00
2-year subscriptions (domestic): $97.00

American Hemlockian Association
New Subscriptions Department
ATTN: Mary Schneider
The Hemlock Building
22345 Connecticut Avenue, N.W.
Washington, DC 20036

Ernst von Krankman, Ph.D.

THE PSEUDO-SCIENCE
BOOK CLUB

The Coalition for the Complete Professional Equality of Everybody (CCPEE) is pleased to announce a new service for those aspiring to professional status—**The Pseudo-Science Book Club**. PSBC will bring you discounted publications designed to help you achieve professional equality with competitors who have been using their education, training, skills, and other credentials to discriminate against you in the provision of services to the paying public.

The Pseudo-Science Book Club offers an outstanding line of quality books to help you achieve professional and financial equality with exclusionary professionals in your community. Here is a sample of some of our forthcoming titles.

God is My Board of Examiners
Milton F. Farnsfellow, D.D.
Philosophers have long cited "natural" law as a higher law than "man's" law. Rev. Farnsfellow gives step-by-step guidance on how to avoid licensing through a religious calling. Chapters include: What is a religious calling, and how to get one; Why preachers don't need licenses; Fees are taxable—church donations ain't; and many others to help you see the light of the "one true faith."
$19.95 or one referral.

Jargon: Talking Like a Professional
Edward C.M.B. Blackeburn, Ed.D.
Every profession has its own language; yours is no exception. This is the complete book of buzz-words for every would-be professional who wants to keep clients coming back for more. Think about it—if they always understand you, they'll think they know as much as you do. It's all here—psychology words, medical phrases, academic cliches. Impress clients, family, friends—even legislators may believe that you're qualified and change your state licensing law. You can't be a professional unless you talk like a professional.
$12.50 or $18.50 with a phonetic pronunciation guide.

Nontraditional Education: PSBC Rates the Mills
by the PSBC Consumer Editors.
Tired of colleagues who put you down because you don't have the right alphabet after your name? You can get any degree you want, without paying hundreds of dollars to the expensive, well-known degree mills and spending valuable hours writing a book report to fulfill their doctoral requirements. This consumer service book lists every nontraditional degree in the free world. Includes tips like—resume writing to reflect "life ex-

perience," why a degree from a smaller, less expensive and less well-known institution may be better than a doctorate costing $500 from a well-known mill, and what types of parchments most impress potential clients. Ph.D., Ed.D., Go.D.—get your advanced degree now. Certificate for 10 Continuing Education credits included.
$24.99 (Special—Buy now and get *High School at Home* at no extra charge.)

Folio Affiliation Analysis
Mary C. Smith, M.S., and Helen D. Smith-Bracken, Ph.D.
Folio Affiliation Analysis is *the* up and coming science. Assess and diagnose client's mental problems by the kind of house plants they keep, or the shrubs they prefer. Treat problems by changing the foliage around the client. Includes case histories of a man cured of impotence by planting royal palm trees in his yard, and a woman whose aggressive tendencies disappeared when her venus fly traps were removed. A real profit center for therapists with a friend in the nursery business.
$16.98 (loose leaf).

Be Your Own Sexual Surrogate
Dr. X.
Pending outcome of his current legal problems, we can't use our author's name—but you'd be surprised! This book tells you how to increase profits by serving as a sexual surrogate for your clients. Covers: How to obtain clients attractive enough to benefit from your services; Which clients won't violate your confidentiality; Avoiding legal and ethical pitfalls (currently under revision).
$9.95 or the equivalent in cigarettes, delivered.

These are just some of the exciting, interesting, and profitable books that you will enjoy by joining **The Pseudo-Science Book Club**

-------------------------------- **JOIN TODAY!!!** --------------------------------

Yes! Enroll me in **The Pseudo-Science Book Club**. I agree to buy at least 7 books per month and to not cancel my membership for at least 5 years. In addition, I can get one free selection for every person I help to enroll in **The Pseudo-Science Book Club**.

Name _____

Address _____

City _____ State _____ Zip _____

Mail to: **The Pseudo-Science Book Club**, The Life Experience University of the Eastern Seaboard, c/o Milt's Bar & Grill, Key West, FL 33040.

☐ Check enclosed.

☐ Please charge to my
   Visa   MC   AE   DC
   Card # _____
   Expiration date_____

☐ Please bill me.

Raibeart Dunbar MacDonald, M. Ed.

Journal of Anorexia Nervosa:
Theory, Research, & Practice

The Trustees of Anorectics Anonymous are extremely pleased to announce[1] the **Journal of Anorexia Nervosa: Theory, Research, & Practice**. Now completing its first year of publication, the journal is the official publication of Anorectics Anonymous (AA), a non-for-profit fellowship of men and women (particularly women) devoted to self-help with the problem of anorexia nervosa.

The **Journal of Anorexia Nervosa: Theory, Research, & Practice** is devoted to the publication of only the very, very, very best material on the topic of eating disorders. Under the direction of Dr. Cynthia Overton, herself a recovered anorectic, and now a leading proponent of the anorexia nervosa self-help

---

[1] As the Trustees of Anorectics Anonymous, we were very concerned about the publication of such an enormous-sized advertisement as this one, fearing that others might perceive us as overdoing publicity for our organization. However, after much soul searching, we decided that outreach is a critical component of our organization and therefore a huge advertisement such as this was indeed justified.

movement, the journal has gone in its very first year from a somewhat unwieldy 160-pages per issue to a slimmed down, more manageable, attractive, pleasing, and readable 96-pages per issue. Although we do anticipate that there may be some further fluctuations in the length of the periodical from issue to issue, Dr. Overton has expressed a strong commitment to keeping the material to exactly 96 pages or under.

The **Journal of Anorexia Nervosa: Theory, Research, & Practice** welcomes the submission of manuscripts for publication. Because of the journal's editorial aim of showcasing as many high quality, original theoretical and research papers as possible within the boundaries set by the somewhat limited page count, prospective authors must keep their manuscripts to no longer than 2 1/2 pages in length. (Papers longer than 2 1/2 pages will be edited down to 2 1/2 pages or less.) Where quality of manuscripts is concerned, the journal holds to some of the most demanding standards in the publishing field today—publishing only 1 out of every 102 manuscripts submitted. While this quest for perfect or, perhaps more realistically, very near-perfect manuscripts has at times resulted in a drastic shortage of material for publication, and even once or twice required the temporary suspension or delay of a few issues of the journal, this certainly has not proved to be a problem, since readers have simply been given the clear message that the journal's high standards afford them the very best articles that could be had for their subscription dollars.

Special Subscription Offer:

Subscribe now for a 1-year subscription and receive for free the pocket-size, clear-laminated, washable, and stain-resistant Anorectics Anonymous' Official Calorie Counter Card. Subscribe for 2-years and receive the Waist-Master™, a special digital weight scale calibrated in ounces.

Subscription Price:

1 Year	2 Years
$112.00	$156.00
32.75	59.00
56.00	81.00
63.56	98.23

Journal of Anorexia Nervosa
c/o Anorectics Anonymous
1024 Round-kitchen Hill
Hershey, PA 15211

Seymour Fruitlooper, Ph.D.

11
Book Reviews

A Book Review of Three Contemporary Popular Psychology Books:
Men Who Hate Women and the Women Who Love Them; Men Who Can't Love; and Women Men Love, Women Men Leave

Michael F. Shaughnessy, Ph.D.
Eastern New Mexico University

Men Who Hate Women and the Women Who Love Them
Dr. Susan Forward and Joan Torres, Bantam, 1986,
$16.95 hardcover

Men Who Can't Love
Steven Carter and Julia Sokol, Evans, 1987,
$14.95 hardcover

Women Men Love, Women Men Leave
Dr. Connell Cowan and Dr. Melvyn Kinder, Crown, 1987,
$18.95 hardcover

Typically, in a book review section, books are reviewed independently. However, a plethora of relevant books on interpersonal relationships have appeared and in the interest of brevity the above three books will be reviewed conjointly.

These books deal with women who hate men and the men who love them, in addition to the men who hate women, and the men who love them. Of particular interest is the women who can't love and the men and women who love them. Further, there are men whom women love and the men women leave, as well as the women whom women love and the men whom women leave, as well as the women whom men leave. There are, of course, women who can't love, but can't leave men, and the men women can't leave.

The authors address the issues of leaving men who can't love, and the inability of leaving women who hate men. Therapists will find assistance in helping women who can't love men and gain insight into the hating of men who can't love as well as the loving of women who can't love or leave.

Loving or leaving, take it or leave it, these books offer profound, salient insights into the leaving and loving of men and women who either can't love, can't leave, or can't be left. Don't be left out on the understanding of women that women love to hate, as well as the women that women love to leave, as well as the women that women hate to love, as well as the women that women hate to leave.

The authors address the issues of leaving and loving, living and learning, and hating and loving. These books fill a major void in the psychology of loving and leaving, and hating and leaving. Those who desire insight into the women men hate, the men who love them, the women who can't love, leave, or hate, and the men women love and the men women leave, will be very inspired by these pages. Those therapists who work with women who hate women, men who hate men, women women love, and women women leave, as well as men women love and leave, as well as leave and love, will be richly rewarded by the wisdom in these pages.

These authors anticipate a new series of books shortly on ambivalence, under similar titles.

12
Contemporary Issues
in Psychology

Learned Lawlessness: Subversion of the Rule of Law by the Eastern Psychological Association (EPA)

Steven J. Gilbert , Ph.D.
State University of New York at Oneonta

Learned Lawlessness is an orientation induced by participation in systems which maintain rules but do not enforce them. The author uncovers the sordid history and dangerous effects of the failure of the Eastern Psychological Association (EPA) to enforce its 50-word Short Abstract rule. Remedies are suggested.[1]

The bicentennial of the United States Constitution has engendered in many of us a sense of sadness for what we have lost. Inexorably slipping away is the shared acceptance of the Rule of Law—the principle that we obey specific laws we do not like in order to support a larger system of laws that on balance works to our benefit. Adherence to this rule requires a somewhat advanced level of ego and moral development (Freud, 1962; Kohlberg & Candee, 1984), a touch of the belief in a Just World (Lerner & Miller, 1978), and the availability of significant others who model restraint (Bandura, 1965). These conditions appear to be dwindling.

The current decline in law-abiding behavior also reflects changes in contingencies of reinforcement operating in American society. Increasingly, rewards for rule-following behavior are omit-

---

[1]*Editor's Note:* Dr. Gilbert should be commended for limiting his abstract to our 50-word rule, with 3 words to spare. We do, however, plan to abandon this rule in the near future.

ted, and punishments for rule-violating behavior are not applied. Instead, we find unbridled competition providing rewards to those who break rules, and punishing the ever smaller minority who continue to follow them. The result of the failure of institutions to enforce their rules is that more and more people are internalizing an orientation that might be called Learned Lawlessness.

One of the primary contributors to Learned Lawlessness in the United States is the Eastern Psychological Association (EPA). Each Year EPA sponsers a convention and invites psychologists to submit papers. The specified format for submission includes a 50-word "Short Abstract" for inclusion in the *Proceedings and Abstracts* provided to all who attend the convention. Preparing such an abstract is a most difficult task, requiring skill, patience, perseverance, and acceptance of an imperfect self-presentation. But the activity also has its rewards: pride in meeting a challenge, the learning of an important discipline, the strengthening of the will, and purification through obedience.

Operating under the natural and presumably intended assumption that submission of a 50- (or fewer) word Short Abstract is a necessary condition for acceptance of a manuscript, the present author always topped his EPA paper preparations with an assiduous and laborious attempt to prune the Short Abstract to this length. Perhaps it was the particular difficulty he had in reducing his 1986 abstract that sensitized him to the issue of others' compliance with the 50-word rule. Or his growing preoccupation with abnegations of the implicit social contract undergirding Western Civilization. In either case, his first glance at the 1986 *Proceedings and Abstracts* of EPA triggered a realization that the 50-word limit seemed not to have been strictly enforced. He had to know for sure.

In the best tradition of scientific psychology, a random sample of 40 Short Abstracts was chosen (20 for papers and 20 for posters), and the number of words in each was counted. The mean number of words was 87.2 ($SD = 19.34$). Not a single abstract contained 50 or fewer words. Indeed, the author's entry on page 73 (Gilbert, Downing, Gould, & Guzy, 1986) appears to be the only 50-word abstract in the entire book!

A number of implications flow from this fact. First are those affecting the author. His abstract looks skimpy when viewed in the context of the other abstracts on page 73—a phenomenon likely exacerbated by a contrast effect (Sherif & Hovland, 1961). The abstract's perceived puniness, in turn, may have fueled a halo effect (Thorndike, 1920), moving conference attendees to the inference that the author's work lacks substance, and that the author himself probably is a dullard, incapable of finding 87 good words to say about his own research.

In light of these processes, many EPA participants may have decided to avoid the author's (Sunday, 1:15 P.M.) presentation, opting instead for the "meatier" presentations suggested by the longer abstracts of competing authors. Such an exigency would have resulted in a greatly reduced distribution of copies of the author's paper, both at the conference, and later, through redistribution at attendees' universities and agencies. A significantly diminished total readership not only would reduce the potential for prosocial impact of the author's work, but also could constrict career advancement opportunities which appreciative readings of the author's paper (by persons with influence in high places) might have precipitated. Thus, opportunities lost, both to psychological science and the author's career, as a function of the nonenforcement of the 50-word abstract rule by EPA, almost certainly were considerable.

But there is a more important issue here than the suppression of one man's work, or the tarnishing of his career by EPA. By encouraging massive violation of an explicitly stated rule, EPA has contributed substantively to the escalating scourge of Learned Lawlessness which rapidly is reaching critical mass in our society. Each time a person succeeds through an act of lawbreaking, the meaning, emotional significance, and inhibitory potential of such acts are deflated (Krugman, 1965), both for the self and for others observing the self (Gerwitz & Stingle, 1968). Breaking into EPA with an illicit 120-word abstract today easily gradates into cheating on Income Tax or writing cigarette advertisements tomorrow. How many this very day wistfully lament, "If only EPA hadn't accepted that overlong Short Abstract I settled for because I didn't have Steve Gilbert's integrity or fear of rejection, I never would have gotten into. . . ." The readers can fill in the rest for themselves.

A system suffering from Learned Lawlessness spawned by unenforced rules can move in two directions—it can mobilize an effort at enforcement (back to the threshold of effective intermittent punishment), or it can abandon its rules. The former option is costly and painful, but there is a long-term payoff, and it is great: the reinstitution of the social contract upon which civilized life depends. The second option has a single virtue: Another layer of the societal veil of hypocrisy is lifted. But behind the veil lurks anarchy, nihilism, fratricide, totalitarianism, tyranny, and the final destruction of the human spirit. This is the option recently embraced by EPA.

The latest EPA announcement of its 59th Annual Meeting omits any reference to the previous 50-word limit for its Short Abstract. Any abstract which can be fitted into the space allotted in "Short Abstract Form" now is acceptable (100 words can easily be squeezed into this space). For first-time EPA convention aspirants, this simply means that a stimulus for development of discipline and pride (i.e., the required cleansing of a product contaminated by self-indulgent length) will have been missed.

For veteran EPA entrants, the sudden disappearance of the 50-word limit has the additional consequence of reiterating the perception that communal flouting of a legitimate but demanding rule eventually precipitates the withdrawal of the rule. The result is another decrement in the societal pool of internalized capacity to initiate and sustain activities which are painful, but necessary to the common good. In addition, EPA's action encourages psychohistorical revisionism, whereby the laudable efforts of those who previously had struggled to comply with the 50-word limit are seen, instead, as pathetic reflections of neurotic or authoritarian personality structures, which we know is definitely not true.

The present author suggests that EPA adopt the first (Enforcement) solution to the 50-word Short Abstract violation problem. A "strong form" of the Enforcement Solution would involve three steps. First, EPA should reinstate the 50-word Short Abstract rule and then reject every entry which supplies a Short Abstract of greater than 50 words; the rejection should be communicated in a note explaining simply that "the Short Abstract violates the 50-word rule and therefore is rejected." Second, the venue of the conference should be moved to the EPA Executive Officer's home, where the seven accepted papers can be read in an atmosphere of congeniality and a setting appropriate to the meeting's scale. Third, a task force should be organized to locate all prior submissions to EPA containing Short Abstracts of 50 or fewer words which nevertheless had been rejected. These papers can be matched with accepted papers dealing with similar issues containing Short Abstracts with more than 50 words. Revised *Annual Proceedings* books then can be published and distributed to all EPA members (past and present, free of charge) with the rightful (but rejected) entries restored to their appropriate positions and the offensive pretenders deleted.

A weaker version of the Enforcement Solution might eliminate the third action (which could be considered somewhat costly). Also, a well-constituted task force might find some alternative ways to restore the legitimacy and prosocial potential of EPA that avoid a few of the possible pitfalls of the first and second actions. Whatever solution finally is adopted, there should be no mistaking that the stakes are very high: The fabric of our Judeo-Christian heritage nearly has been torn asunder, and the resolve of EPA to restore its strand may be decisive. The challenge is clear. In the words of the great Rabbi Hillel: If not EPA, who? If not now, when?

References

Bandura, A. (1965). Influence of model's reinforcement contingencies on the acquisition of imitative responses. *Journal of Personality and Social Psychology, 1,* 589–595.

Freud, S. (1962). *The ego and the id.* New York: W. W. Norton.

Gerwitz, J. L., & Stingle, K. G. (1968). Learning of generalized limitation as the basis for identification. *Psychological Review, 75,* 374–397.

Gilbert, S. J., Downing, L., Gould, F., & Guzy, L. (1986). *Mandating seatbelt use: Effects on behavior and attitudes.* Paper presented at the meeting of the Eastern Psychological Association, New York City.

Kohlberg, L., & Candee, D. (1984). The relationship of moral judgment to moral action. In W. M. Kurtines & J. L. Gerwitz (Eds.), *Morality, moral behavior, and moral development.* New York: Wiley.

Krugman, H. E. (1965). The impact of television advertising: Learning without involvement. *Public Opinion Quarterly, 29,* 349–356.

Lerner, M. J., & Miller, D. T. (1978). Just world research and the attribution process: Looking back and ahead. *Psychological Bulletin, 85,* 1030–1051.

Sherif, M., & Howland, C. I. (1961). *Social judgment: Assimilation and contrast effects in communication and attitude change.* New Haven: Yale University Press.

Thorndike, E. I. (1920). A constant error in psychological rating. *Journal of Applied Psychology, 4,* 25–29.

Pathological Lying: An Important—No, the Most Important Clinical Problem Facing Mental Health Professionals

David O. Antonuccio, Ph.D., William G. Danton, Ph.D., Blake H. Tearnan, Ph.D., and Kathy Alberding, M.S.W.
V. A. Medial Center at Reno

We have written an article—no, several articles on pathological lying. Actually we've coauthored a book—a *series* of books on the subject. Yea, that's it. Pathological lying is a serious—no, the most serious problem facing clinicians today (Trustme, 1985). We have developed a treatment program which helps 50%, 60%, or even 100% of patients to overcome their problem with lying.

Our theory postulates that lying is an avoidance response to phobic anxiety of the truth. The treatment approach we have developed involves flooding the patient with the truth until his/her anxiety abates.

A clinical example involved a patient we shall refer to as John. John was a 40-year-old white man who was employed as a gaffer on a tuna boat—actually, he was the captain on a fishing boat—in fact, if I remember correctly he was the owner of an international fishing fleet. He was referred to our clinic by a rural mental health—rather, a university medical—no, in fact it was President Reagan. Yea, that's it. John was a patho—well, a chronic liar. John originally applied for services in 196—no, 1985; yea, in fact we're sure that was the year because that's the year we all won the Pulitzer—rather, the Nobel prize for helping with the DNA helix project—in our spare time—while we did therapy with John.

Anyway, John came in and said he wanted therapy for some phobia he'd developed. We all agreed to treat him with the latest bioelectrical equipment technique, and even though we told him how expensive this kind of treatment was, he agreed to treatment no matter how expensive and no matter how long it took and no matter what we did. Needless to say we had no idea he'd later deny all this and claim *we* lied! Anyway, John insisted on two appointments per day, and even though we were plenty busy we agreed to that. We figured the Kennedys could just wait until John's treatment was concluded.

John's primary presenting problem was that he compulsively lied about his age. He claimed he was 30 years old when in fact he was actually 40 years old. The treatment consisted of exposing John to the truth about his age. We brought John's mother to the session and she repeated over and over again, "You were born in 1946. I ought to know, I was there. You are 40 years old." We had a copy of his birth certificate which we forced him to read. Finally, we brought in the doctor who delivered him who confirmed the date of his birth. Eventually, John began screaming "All right! I admit it! I'm 40 years old." This admission was maintained through 3—rather, 6 months' follow-up.

This treatment has been successfully utilized in countless other patients with a diagnosis of pathological lying. In fact, this treatment has never failed to result in a complete cure. No kidding!

Reference

Trustme, U. Ken. (1985). Lying: An important—no, the most important clinical problem facing mental health professionals. *Journal of Psychology—No, All Mental Health, 3* (2), 7–16.

Notes

Note 1: This paper has been submitted—no, accepted for publication by the *Journal of Clinical Psychology*—no, *Science*. Yea, that's it.

Note 2: They all lied. We, Carol Vasso and Julie Anderson, the secretaries of the Mental Hygiene Clinic, and Bill Gruzenski and Pat Chatham, the other clinical staff in the Mental Hygiene Clinic, are in truth the real authors of this very important article.

Note 3: No, *they're* lying! They had nothing to do with this article. Nothing! In fact the secretaries weren't even allowed to read what they were typing.

Note 4: Our next article will detail how to ascertain, with only one question, who is lying and who is telling the truth. (It will also include the results of our research on the double helix.)

Changes in Professional and Administrative Practices in the Delivery of Psychological and Psychiatric Services: A Proposal Directed Toward Increasing Our Share of the Health Care Dollar (HC$)

Temps Perdu, Ph.D., and Paul M. Brinich, Ph.D.
Case Western Reserve University

Attempts to curb the rising cost of health care have led to a rapid contraction in the health care market. This has led, in turn, to changes in professional attitudes and practice which affect clinical psychology as well as the other healing professions. Decisions which formerly were made on purely clinical grounds are now examined with an eye to marketing, competition, and cash flow. This essay suggests how marketing techniques—such as the use of designer-endorsed treatment programs, marketed through national franchises—could revolutionize the mental health field and lead us into a brave new era in which our services would become as easily available as fast food, with similar effects upon their quality.

Changes in the mental health marketplace are occurring at an ever-increasing pace. Dominant among these changes are those initiated by the various third-party payors—both private and public—aimed at decreasing the cost of health services generally and mental health services specifically. Costs are being decreased by (1) limiting *types* of reimbursed services, (2) limiting covered *diagnoses*, (3) limiting *length* of service (especially of hospitalization), and (4) increasing *co-payment* requirements in ways that discourage the use of mental health services.

In this increasingly competitive atmosphere, mental health facilities must take a proactive, aggressive stance aimed at preserving or increasing their share of the health care market. We would like to suggest some changes in professional and administrative practices which, we believe, will give a "new look"—and a new fiscal vitality—to mental health in the next decade. We have grouped our suggestions into several areas: product diversity and enhancement, administrative practices, and marketing.

Product Diversity and Enhancement

Increased product diversity is one way to maintain or increase mental health's share of the Health Care Dollar (HC$). Mental health practitioners must develop novel programs which will attract some of the large number of *healthy* people who are currently seriously underserved by the health care industry.

Examples that have already proven their economic muscle are (1) programs that promise to turn anyone into a real estate millionaire in a matter of weeks through judicious application of the power of positive thinking and multiple credit cards; (2) programs that frighten affluent parents with statistics about adolescent drug use and then promise to save their children from these dangers; and (3) programs that promise to turn working mothers into guilt-free super-moms capable of leading successful professional and domestic lives. These programs already *exist*; the task is simply to make them *reimbursible!*

The time is ripe for a return to techniques which offer quick cures for a wide range of symptoms. For example, hypnotherapy, despite a checkered history, remains an attractive treatment modality in the eye of the lay public. If this modality could be combined with other incentives—for example, a Caribbean cruise—some leisure and vacation dollars could be redirected into mental health. Given truly skilled hypnotists, it should be possible to substitute a trip on the Staten Island Ferry for the Caribbean cruise; this would reduce treatment overhead substantially.

Another approach to product diversity is the creation of a small number of "designer" treatments, with premium fees. Jane Fonda might sponsor an eating disorders program and Betty Ford already has her own alcoholism program (which could be franchised nationally). Recent marketing studies suggest that a "Marilyn Monroe Center for the Treatment of Depression" or a "Howard Hughes Paranoia Program" would both attract a very select clientele. (The latter two programs have the additional advantage that no licensing fee need be paid.)

Products must be developed to serve neglected groups of consumers, for example, (1) those who have not yet been born and (2) those who have already died. Although these groups represent the vast majority of the people who will ever live, *currently less than 1% of the health care dollar is spent on these groups!* While it is not clear how the mechanics of reimbursement by third-party payors would be worked out, it is easy to imagine products and programs which might focus on these groups.

For example, there are many childhood disorders (e.g., Attention Deficit Disorder) which are statistically associated with prenatal factors. Fetal monitors and biofeedback devices make the task of teaching fetuses to attend to extrauterine stimuli a relatively trivial one. Fetuses could be taught to increase their attention spans; this would tend to reduce the likelihood of a later Attention Deficit Disorder.

Such a preventive intervention could be marketed with a money-back guarantee, enhancing the consumer-responsive image of the mental health profession. And even if the techniques proved to be ineffective, some minor actuarial adjustments could keep them profitable since the incidence of true Attention Deficit Disorder is quite low.

At the other end of the spectrum are those patients who have already died. Mental health practitioners have much to learn from their mortician colleagues in the development of profitable products designed to serve these consumers and their families.

Diversification offers protection against some of the ups and downs of consumer demand. Mental health facilities might market insurance against specific DSM-III diagnoses, with premiums and benefits tailored to fit special subgroups. Affluent subscribers might purchase insurance against a major depression, with benefits including long-term psychoanalytic treatment. Less affluent subscribers might prefer policies that provide lower-cost or "token" treatment (e.g., brief psychotherapy, chemotherapy, and electroconvulsive therapy).

Diversification should include the conversion of current facilities to new uses. Some waiting-room space could be remodeled into a Mental Health Gift Shop (or "Head Shop") where patients could purchase items related to their specific needs. Both defenses against fears (e.g., amulets to ward off poisonous spiders) and fear-eliciting stimuli (e.g., live tarantulas) could be available. Therapists might prescribe specific items for purchase. Gift certificates might also be available; these would be especially popular items around Mother's Day, Father's Day, and anniversaries. Greeting cards could be designed to reflect the different theoretical orientations of specific treatments. Bumper stickers advertising the therapeutic efficacy of specific treatments could be distributed *gratis* or sold. Any remaining unused waiting-room space could be turned into profitable use with coin-operated tanning equipment, washing machines, or video games.

If some of these suggestions seem ahead of their time, we would urge you to look around at what other health care specialists have already accomplished. Large medical centers offer hotels, travel agencies, and clerical or security staff to attend to the needs of their most valuable customers. Groups of obstetricians operate boutiques which sell designer-label maternity clothes. Physiatrists are partners in sporting goods stores, exercise clubs, and Arthur Murray dance studios. Mental health professionals have fallen behind the times.

Administrative Practices

Administration holds the key to the profitability of mental health facilities. The truly important decisions affecting the quality of clinical care now are made at the administrative level. Imaginative administrators will be able to see beyond current patterns of practice to new, more efficient and profitable service delivery.

For example, cooperative business practices could ensure that all referrals for health care remained within a limited group of providers while *informal* administrative arrangements discouraged overuse of scarce resources.

The limitation of referrals described above would, if pursued aggressively, quickly bankrupt any private practitioners who attempted to retain their independence. Once private practice was no longer a viable option, administrators could renegotiate the compensation of therapists to reflect the weakened bargaining position of the individual provider.

Administration could also set up consumer credit subsidiaries which would help consumers meet the costs of health care. Credit insurance would ensure that patients did not evade payment of their accounts by dying. (This would be a requirement for suicidal patients.)

Administration should also give attention to details of geography and scheduling. Satellite offices at upscale shopping malls (especially those with a Bloomingdale's or Saks branch store) could offer flexible scheduling with beepers available to notify customers that their therapist would be free to see them in 10 minutes.

Cooperative arrangements with other professionals would allow shared use of basic facilities, leading to increased productivity for all. Dentists are an obvious choice since they already have couches in place and many of their consumers are very anxious. "Family Mental/Dental Centers" may, in fact, be the wave of the future in mental health.

Profitability requires careful monitoring of variations in the utilization of specific treatments. Since major depressions are relatively infrequent in times of good weather, a two-for-one special on electroconvulsive therapy might be offered during summer months. Manufacturers of specific products (e.g., neuroleptic medications) might be asked to subsidize specific services in return for introducing consumers to the manufacturers' products. Coupons and mail-in rebates offer tax write-offs while they encourage consumers to try treatments which may be lagging in their contributions to institutional cash flow.

A final area for creative administration has to do with links between major health care providers and corporations such as Scandinavian Health Spas and General Nutrition. Such links offer the increased efficiency of both horizontal and vertical integration and will ensure that health care dollars remain where they belong regardless of the state of health of the consumer. In addition, consumers who are injured can be referred back to the parent corporation very efficiently.

Marketing

Mental health administrators have been slow to recognize the miracles of modern marketing. This, however, is changing: Sears Roebuck now offers, through its "Discover" credit card division, a 50% discount on psychiatric evaluations done at Hospital Corporation of America psychiatric facilities. This, however, is only the beginning.

Frequent user cards, modeled after frequent flyer cards, could offer consumers special incentives to maintain their brand loyalty. Psychiatric hospitals which offered recuperative care in Tahiti following inpatient treatment for depression would find themselves hard-pressed to meet the demand created. (Treatment outcome might also improve.) Special interest rates, manufacturer's rebates on prosthetic devices, and free gifts upon the payment of all outstanding bills are other ways of influencing the consumer's choice of a mental health facility.

Guarantees of results, while somewhat more risky, also have their place in any broad marketing strategy. While no mental health treatment has yet been awarded the *Good Housekeeping* Seal of Approval, this is only a matter of time. Warranties covering parts and/or labor are common in many other segments of the marketplace; mental health facilities have not kept pace.

Creative marketing also includes direct reinforcement of desired consumer response. Presenting each consumer with a lottery ticket at the end of each treatment session would quickly cut down on cancellations and missed appointments. A lottery terminal at the registration desk would also increase general consumer traffic. The addition of a bar and grill would allow the institution to provide services to compulsive gamblers, to substance abusers, and to overeaters in a single, cost-effective location. What is more, treatment "failures" would contribute as much as treatment successes to the fiscal health of the institution.

The variable reinforcement schedule of a lottery might be augmented by a fixed reinforcement schedule which awarded medals, T-shirts, or other premiums to patients for consistency in attendance, for amount of therapeutic improvement, for referral of new patients, and so on. Ten consecutive "kept" appointments might lead to a merit badge; consumers who participate in several different types of treatment might eventually achieve the rank of "Explorer."

Finally, we need to recognize that, in many cases, our "consumers" are no longer individual people but are employers or labor unions who are as interested as we are in the "bottom line." Since our loyalty must, in the final analysis, lie with those who pay the bills, it is clear that the future of mental health resides in the board rooms, *not* in the consultation rooms. Outmoded concepts such as the "doctor-patient relationship" must be replaced by new concepts which emphasize the mutually rewarding relationship between fiscal officers on both sides of the health care "fence."

Conclusion

There are many ways in which mental health facilities can improve and diversify their product lines, increase their market shares, decrease their costs, and increase their fees. All of this hinges upon one crucial factor: administration. Mental health facilities need more well-qualified, imaginative, and well-paid administrators at *every* level of organization. Outpatient clinics, divisions such as child psychiatry, disciplines such as nursing, social work, and psychology—each must have its own administrator if each component is to contribute to the overall goal of the institution. These administrators must be ready and willing to provide leadership, able to make the tough decisions that clinically oriented personnel sometimes avoid.

Indeed, administrative skills are much more crucial than clinical skills if mental health facilities are to move to a position of leadership in the wider health care market. It is only a matter of time before an MBA degree will be a prerequisite for any position with significant clinical responsibility. Some psychiatric residency programs have already recognized this and include course work in business administration as well as more traditional clinical training. These will be the leaders of tomorrow!

In order to function efficiently as a team, these administrators must be organized into levels (i.e., Presidents, Vice Presidents) which accurately reflect their contributions to the team. They also need secretarial, clerical, and computer support to ensure that policy planning can be responsive to new market opportunities.

Finally, it is essential that these administrative policy makers be thoroughly shielded from any clinical issues which might cloud their vision.

From all that has been said, it might seem that the demand for administrators would quickly outstrip the supply. Experience tells a far different, happier tale. Administrators tend to appear as quickly as they are needed (and often even sooner). Once they appear, they are extraordinarily loyal; they will not abandon their positions until every other position has been cut. Even then they usually only retreat to higher ground, where they continue to contribute to the policy making activities of their institution.

As mental health facilities face the end of the 20th century and ponder their entry into a newer, more imaginative and more competitive era, they might do well to remember Benjamin Franklin's words to John Hancock: "We must indeed all hang together, or, most assuredly, we shall all hang separately." Given sufficient product diversity, aggressive marketing, and creative administrative guidance we are sure to hang together.

The Write Stuff: II. A Grammatical Overview of Social Service Recipients' Correspondence

Robert W. Mitchell, A.C.S.W.

In his article "A Grammatical Overview of Medical Records: The Write Stuff," Fox (1986) illustrated that when it comes to clear and effective writing abilities, medical personnel have much "room for growth." Medical professionals, however, are not the only ones who fail to communicate exactly what they mean; social service recipients, too, are oftentimes guilty of less than ideal grammatical constructions. As an example, the following quotes were extracted from letters written to a large metropolitan welfare department.

1. In answer to your letter, I have given birth to a boy weighing ten pounds. This I hope is satisfactory.
2. Please find out for certain if my husband is dead. The man I am living with can't eat or do anything until he knows.
3. I cannot get sick pay. I have six children. Can you tell me why?
4. I am forwarding my marriage certificate and six children. I had seven but one died which was baptized on a half sheet of paper.
5. I am very much annoyed to find that you have branded my son illegitimate. This is a dirty lie as I was married a week before he was born.
6. Unless I get my husband's money pretty soon, I will be forced to lead an immortal life.
7. You have changed my little boy to a girl. Will this make any difference?

8. My husband got his project cut off two months ago and I haven't had any relief since.
9. In accordance with your instructions, I have given birth to twins in the enclosed envelope.
10. I want money as quick as I can get it. I have been in bed with the doctor for two weeks and he doesn't do me any good. If things don't improve, I will have to send for another doctor.

Reference

Fox, C. D. (1986). A grammatical overview of medical records: The write stuff. *Journal of Polymorphous Perversity*, 3(1), 6.

Hospital Privileges for Psychologists with the Write Stuff: Medical Records Revisited

Jeri J. Goldman, Ph.D.

Utilizing the records of an urban general hospital, Fox (1986) attempted to illustrate the expertise of the hospital's medical staff. As the present examples demonstrate, however, the grammatical training of psychologists equally qualifies them for hospital privileges, thus providing the patient with freedom of choice in bloopers, gaffs, and other integral aspects of creative writing so necessary to thorough and efficient care.

Deftly and definitively, psychologists have the requisite skills necessary to:

Take Case Histories

When she was young she felt that everyone stared at her because of her lack of clothes.

Patient was blue at birth and did not cry for three to five minutes after conception.

Epilepsy, venerable disease, etc. were denied.

Penicillin makes Nanette regurgitate—has to wear oral retainers.

There are other significant problems in the family that lend cretins to Larry's opinions.

Provide Careful Clinical Descriptions

The patient has a limited extension span.

David especially enjoyed the second teat session.

Examination was arrempted bust incomplete because of patient irresistance.

Harry was well manured throughout this activity.

Tim becomes quite confussed in spelling.

The patient knows something is wrong with him but does not know how to cope with his affirmity.

She is pregnant now and the doctor wonders what may develop.

Establish Definitive Diagnoses

The patient is diagnosed as having an involutional melancholia in acute exasperation.

The patient has a passive-offensive personality, antisocial type.

Jerome is described as a multiply handicapped child with a diagnosis of evasive developmental disorder.

She has been diagnosed as having diffused brain damage.

I think the difference in verbal and performance scores is organic enough to be functional.

Mental ability: Absent.

Offer Astute Treatment and Recommendations

Attending psychiatrist strongly recommends impatient care for this very difficult girl.

The following is a report of weekly grope therapy on the ward.

This woman is obsessed with rape fantasies. However, she can be very seductive herself, and at one time took off all her clothes and ran naked through the ward. I hope this may give you some idea of the problems you may fun into in treating this patient.

Recommendation: Refer back to spychologist.

This case may become a court matter. Mr. . . . , attorney, has threatened to subpoena the clinic records. Dr. . . . , suggests that the caseworker dispose of the patient as quickly as possible.

When there are last minute changes in case conferences, everyone concerned should be notified ahead of time.

Engage in Informative Public Information Services

Suicide has become a grave problem among today's teenagers. For ethical as well as legal reasons, psychologists insure that patients authorize the relief of records.

The . . . , with some 3,700 employees, is the largest employer of the rapists in the nation, with the exception of federal government agencies.

The Center is a non-profit rehabilitation agency which provides residential and vocational services to chronically, metally ill adults.

Sociologists and social workers have contributed their share of insights, and a few psychiatrists have published their findings, but surprisingly little attention has been devoted to the problem of child abuse by the psychologist.

Conclusion

Psychologists have clearly established themselves as qualified to compete on an equal footing with medical practitioners in the exacting art of professional writing. As the above examples illustrate, these highly trained professionals need defer to no one in their devotion to the motto so well expressed by Thurber (1940, p. 39): "Don't get it right, just get it written."

References

Fox, C. D. (1986). A grammatical overview of medical records: The write stuff. *Journal of Polymorphous Perversity*, 3(1), 6.

Thurber, J. (1940). *Fables for our time and famous poems illustrated.* New York: Harper & Brothers.

About the Editor

GLENN C. ELLENBOGEN is a clinical psychologist who was reared in New Rochelle and Mamaroneck, NY. He went on to New York University for a bachelor's degree in psychology and continued in the graduate program. After completing the master's degree program at New York University, he earned another master's and a doctorate in clinical psychology at Hofstra University. He trained as a clinical intern at Kings County Hospital/Downstate Medical Center, was a post-doctoral fellow at a psychoanalytic training institute in New York City, and was a staff psychologist at Jersey City Medical Center. In 1980 he founded Wry-Bred Press, a small, humor-oriented publishing house and in 1984 he launched the *Journal of Polymorphous Perversity*®, a humorous and satirical magazine spoofing psychology and psychiatry. Ellenbogen lives in New York City with his wife.